CONFESSIONS OF A
SERIAL ENTREPRENEUR

For my mentors. My accomplishments are a testament to their talent and generosity.

JB JOSSEY-BASS

Confessions
of a Serial Entrepreneur

WHY I CAN'T STOP STARTING OVER

Stuart Skorman
with Catherine Guthrie

BICENTENNIAL

1807
WILEY
2007

BICENTENNIAL

John Wiley & Sons, Inc.

338.0973
.S56
2007

831498

Library of Congress Cataloging-in-Publication Data

Skorman, Stuart.
    Confessions of a serial entrepreneur : why I can't stop starting over / by Stuart Skorman, with Catherine Guthrie.
        p. cm.
    Includes index.
    ISBN-13: 978-0-7879-8732-9
    1. Skorman, Stuart. 2. Businesspeople—United States—Biography. 3. New business enterprises—United States. I. Guthrie, Catherine S. II. Title.
    HC102.5.S424A3 2007
    338.0973092—dc22
    [B]   2006036473

Printed in the United States of America
FIRST EDITION
HB Printing   10 9 8 7 6 5 4 3 2 1

CONTENTS

Introduction   1

1   My Jewish Merchant Family   9

*My home town was never home. Thank heaven for
Life magazine.*

2   Sex, Drugs, and the Business of Rock-and-Roll   23

*Some went to business school; I managed a rock band.
(Guess who had more fun?)*

3   Bankruptcy at Home   39

How I tried and failed to save my father's business.

4   Helping to Invent Whole Foods   47

*Battles with my mentor made me wiser, confident,
and determined never to work for anybody again.*

5   Bike-Touring Adventures   63

*By the end of my cross-country journey, I'd decided to
become an entrepreneur.*

6   Building a Video Empire   71

My perfect start-up: a hole-in-the-wall video store.

7   Millionaire Without a Mission   93

*I struck a deal with Blockbuster, headed for Silicon Valley,
and left small-town retail behind forever.*

8   My Professional Poker Career   105

*After two years of high-stakes poker, I was ready
for anything.*

9   Easy Dot Come: The Making of an Internet Pioneer   121

*How I founded and sold a company for $100 million
in less than three years.*

10   Easy Dot Go: Getting Carried Away with the Internet   141

*Good intentions but a lousy business plan is a great way
to lose millions.*

11   Adventures in the Wild   151

*The sharks of the South Pacific are as dangerous
as the ones in Silicon Valley.*

12   Taming a Wild Elephant   161

*I thought I was ready for the biggest project of my life;
now I'm not so sure.*

13   What It Takes (and Doesn't Take) to Be   183
an Entrepreneur

Know yourself, keep learning, and hang on for the ride!

Acknowledgments   195

About the Authors   199

Index   201

Introduction

On the day in November 2002 when Elephant Pharmacy opened, I could hardly contain my excitement. This massive pharmacy in Berkeley, California, was truly original. Elephant was the only store in the industry with two pharmacies under one roof: a prescription pharmacy for Western drugs and an herbal pharmacy for Eastern remedies. And that's not all. You could buy the prescriptions and over-the-counter drugs you'd find at any traditional pharmacy. But you could also buy organic snacks, attend a free yoga class, get a chair massage, browse aisles of natural body care products, peruse a library of wellness books, and even talk to an alternative health practitioner.

Elephant Pharmacy was my latest venture, and it fulfilled my core desire to start a business that was profitable, helped people, and pushed the boundaries of an established industry.

But it was only my most recent venture. During the past thirty-four years, I've started a number of businesses in different industries in various parts of the country. Each time, I introduced a new business model to the industry and strove to enrich my customers' lives in some way. When my business was up and running and growing, I couldn't wait to move on and invent something else.

I can't help myself. I am a serial entrepreneur.

At first glance, the fact that I made a fortune in business may not come as a surprise. I was born into a family of entrepreneurs where each generation bested the one before. My grandfather owned a clothing store in Ravenna, Ohio; my father propelled his business into a regional chain, called Skorman's Miracle Mart; and I have established nationally known companies. I've banked tens of millions of dollars and could have made a billion more if not for mistakes and bad luck.

But to say I set out to follow in my father and grandfather's footsteps couldn't be further from the truth. I didn't want to be a businessman; I yearned to be a poet or a novelist. And I *never* wanted to stay in Ohio.

I was a hyper kid who couldn't focus long enough to make sense of school. I nearly flunked every grade. My floundering didn't go over well at home. The more I failed in the classroom, the more my father, whom I adored, distanced himself from me. I was ostracized and alone.

Then, in 1967, I got a glimpse of the world outside of my midwestern home town. I saw pictures in *Life* magazine of San Francisco's Summer of Love. Hooked by the images of free-spirited hippies, I found a way to spend that summer among them. I went to Haight Street, the epicenter of hippie culture, in search of love, in search of happiness, in search of anything that could take me away from the pain of my childhood. What I found was a lifelong love affair with my generation, the baby boomers.

In this book, you'll read how this hippie wannabe-writer launched the first in a string of successful—and some not so successful—businesses. You'll find out how I learned the nuts and bolts of retail from my Jewish merchant family in Akron, Ohio, and an intimidating Irishman in Cambridge, Massachusetts. You'll read how my chain of Vermont video stores inspired a Silicon Valley dot-com I sold for $100 million.

But my businesses haven't all been successful. One of my dot-coms bombed, and my latest start-up, Elephant Pharmacy, threatened my life savings.

My adventures weren't limited to business. I'm an adrenaline junkie with both my hobbies and my start-ups. When I was drained by the entrepreneurial maelstrom, I sought thrills else-where. Before launching my first dot-com, I spent two years playing high-stakes poker in places likeAtlantic City, Las Vegas, and the Yukon. In my fifties, I traded the sharks of Silicon Valley for the sharks of the South Pacific.

As you read my story, I may look like a wealth-seeking capi-talist; other times I will appear to be an idealistic socialist. Most likely, the truth lies somewhere in between.

My pattern of starting a company and then moving on to the next, over and over again, isn't something I'd recommend to most people, but it suits me, and I've learned a lot in the process. This book contains many business and entrepreneurship les-sons, but as I reflect on my adventures and misadventures in the start-up world, a few key principles stand out.

The first rule is that a large ego is not just good for an entre-preneur; it's necessary. Starting a business is so difficult, wrench-ing, exhilarating, terrifying, and joyous—all at the same time—that it's almost an unnatural act. Who wants to inflict that kind of trauma on themselves? Who wants to expose themselves to that kind of risk? Who wants to throw every ounce of themselves into what may be a futile effort, especially when conventional businesses offer plenty of jobs?

There's no way around it: start-up entrepreneurs are tem-porarily insane. We endure emotional and financial hardship because we don't know what we are doing. Either we're ignorant of the risks or we're arrogant to the point of believing we are immune to failure.

Temporary insanity, however, is not the only mark of an entrepreneur. We also want to make things happen. We are deter-mined to achieve greatness. The essence of an entrepreneur is the diehard belief that we are the only one able to make things happen. We go above and beyond to turn our dreams into reality.

While entrepreneurs have the egos to strive for bigger-than-life achievements, the end goal is hardly the same for everyone. Some entrepreneurs crave giant bank accounts. Others hunger after power—either the power of control or the power of impact.

I yearn to make people happy through commerce. That's what drives, excites, and thrills my ego. I live to see my creations, decisions, and initiatives foster satisfaction and excitement among my customers.

The second lesson I've learned as an entrepreneur is the importance of emotions. Some start-up business books emphasize mechanics: raising money, finding an idea, and marketing the idea. Sure, there are basic steps to learn, and I'll cover them in the following chapters. But before you worry about mechanics, you should steel yourself for the emotional ups and downs that are inherent in the start-up world.

Starting a business is rampant with emotional extremes. Strong emotions push you into the fray and carry you through to the end. But naming your emotions—joy, greed, passion, and fear—isn't enough; you also need to harness them. Under the right circumstances, strong emotions can work in your favor. Emotions are like thoroughbreds; the fastest horse in the world wouldn't win a single race if not for the jockey who is guiding and directing its explosive energy.

Terror is to be expected. Starting a business is terrifying. Let's face it: most entrepreneurs fail. But terror, if you aren't paralyzed by it, can be healthy. Fear forces you to think. Fear of failure pushes you to work harder than you ever thought possible. Let your terror focus and fuel your determination.

Joy is also present when starting a business. Call it happiness, exhilaration, or excitement. All can be helpful, but joy shouldn't be the base of your emotional foundation. Ultimately business decisions need to be grounded in logic, not elation.

Greed is also inherent to starting a business. Human nature is to want. Greed is motivating, but if it consumes you, it will cloud your decision making and set you up for failure.

Passion certainly drives most successful entrepreneurs. If it weren't for passion, few people would bother starting a business. As with all other emotions, passion must be brought under control. No one succeeds by letting passion run wild.

Last but not least is desperation. Most people don't equate being desperate with being an entrepreneur, but I find the two inseparable. Starting a business is often an act of desperation. Entrepreneurs are desperate for success and accomplishment. Desperation pushes us to take huge risks, leave comfort and security behind, and allow a business to consume our lives.

The ability to harness one's ego and emotions are just two must-have qualities of an entrepreneur. Here are some other lessons I've learned along the way:

Don't be afraid to ask for support. Because starting a business is an emotional rollercoaster, you need support. It helps to surround yourself with people who can tell you not to worry about your mistakes. You also need people to tell you to stop being a jerk or to slow down. We all need someone to give us a hard time occasionally. We all need outside perspectives. Asking for help is not being weak; it's being smart.

Be prepared to give up your life. They say, "Start your own business, and be your own boss." It doesn't work like that.

The truth is really the opposite: when you start a business, you become a slave. A business brings constant pressures, risks, and fears. When you start a business, there are no days off; it is always with you.

Learn from your mistakes. Sure, this is a familiar refrain, but it's one you better know how to sing. This book is chock full of my mistakes. My success is rooted in my ability to recognize my blunders, learn from them, and move past them. I hope you'll learn from some of my errors and discover how to learn from yours.

Most important, choose your business based on who you are. Choosing the right business means knowing yourself. There are many paths to success, and no two are alike. You're about to discover the road I forged, but your personality will demand that you choose your own.

That said, all entrepreneurs have certain traits in common. We are strong-willed, hard working, and thrive on risk. Most important, we've chosen our businesses based on our strengths. As an entrepreneur, picking a business is the biggest decision you'll ever make. Ask yourself: Why are you starting a business? Why are you starting this particular business? The answers to these questions will help you chart your destiny.

Being a serial entrepreneur suits my personality, but it's not right for everyone. The start-up world is messy, risky, and intense. If you like structure, logic, comfort, and predictability or if you prefer to focus on one task at a time, the start-up world may not be for you. By writing this book, I want you to learn from my adventures and missteps. I also want to share the fun. I hope you enjoy the ride as much as I have.

My Jewish Merchant Family

My home town was never home.
Thank heaven for Life magazine.

Long before I was old enough to vote or drive, I was dreaming up new businesses. They were the kinds of things a kid would think up, like a business that made airplanes kids could fly or healthy sodas kids could drink whenever they wanted. Like most other little kids with big ideas, I didn't believe my childhood fantasies would come true. Looking back, though, I realize some of my ideas were eerily similar to the businesses I have started as an adult.

My Business Roots

I have my paternal grandfather, Simon Skorman, to thank for both my entrepreneurial spirit and my Ohio roots. As a teenager in 1914, Simon left Russia to join relatives in Cleveland. His first job was peddling pots and pans from a horse-drawn wagon. Before long, he'd saved enough money to open a small store. Although he went on to lose his first store in the depression of 1921, he wasn't dissuaded. Eventually he opened a second, larger store in Ravenna, Ohio, twenty miles east of Akron. Simon chose his location carefully. Ravenna was a burgeoning town but had few businesses to cater to its growing population. Its residents drove to Akron to buy necessities, like clothes and shoes. My grandfather saw a need, and he filled it.

In addition to having a knack for choosing a great location, my grandfather was a creative problem solver. When his store was struggling, he knew his customers should remain unaware, so he shelved empty boxes to make his inventory look more robust. Luckily, he didn't stock empty boxes for long; his business soon grew into a thriving small-town department store.

A tall man with a dignified presence, Simon prided himself on his ability to converse with his customers in their native languages despite the fact that they came from all over the world. He had only three years of formal schooling, but he spoke eight languages. He could chat with his Amish customers in German, speak Polish to the farmers, and pontificate in Yiddish and Hebrew at the synagogue on Saturdays.

Growing Up in Retail

I was born in 1948 and spent my childhood in Akron. My father and his brothers owned a chain of discount stores called Miracle Mart. He believed discount was the future of retailing, and he was right. Twice a month, my father visited New York City's Garment District. He brought back mountains of cheap goods, stacked them from floor to ceiling in his stores (which were converted warehouses), and sold them to Akron's exploding lower-middle class. His customers spilled out of the nearby tire factories and into his stores every afternoon, snatching up everything from bras to bundt pans. Everything looked like a bargain, whether it was or not.

The men in my family were geniuses at brand building and marketing. For instance, to make sure their customers knew Miracle Mart was the cheapest store in town, they charged only a nickel for a bottle of Coca-Cola when the same bottle was a dime everywhere else. Deeply discounting Coke, a product everyone knew the price of, gave customers the impression that everything in the store was a steal.

My father's nickname was Schetzel (Yiddish for *the thinker*), and he spoke to my family in business stream-of-consciousness. In restaurants, he spent mealtimes speculating on the proprietor's profit margins, payroll expenses, and rent. At gas stations, he quizzed the attendants about what grade of gas people bought. If, while driving down the street, we passed a vacant lot, he'd say, "That'd make a great spot for a hamburger place," or "I haven't seen a car wash for five miles. That's what this neighborhood needs: a car wash." He was always right. To talk to my father was to talk business. Like learning how to chew gum or walk, I don't remember a time when I wasn't designing businesses as a means to communicate with him.

My father's sense of humor shone through in everything he touched. One time when he and his brothers were designing a new store, the manager put the pet department next to the fresh meat department. My father saw the black humor in the juxtaposition and left the two side-by-side until the last minute, just to see if anyone else would catch the joke. His humor could also be seen on the store's signs. They read, "Attention shoplifters: Please do your lifting in the big, fancy stores. Our prices are so low, even you can afford to pay cash."

Being Honest Is More Important Than Being Rich

My father exacted a deep pleasure from making people happy. He'd come home from work with stories about how excited customers were with his bargains. Similarly, he went out of his way to help other businessmen. He knew when he opened a new Miracle Mart that it inevitably put someone else's small store out of business. Feeling terrible, he'd go to the doomed establishment and offer the employees jobs at the new Miracle Mart. Then he'd offer to buy the store's inventory at a fair price. He wanted Miracle Mart to be a win-win for everyone.

My father also taught me about good values. When he learned that a store manager was selling huge numbers of fans by demonstrating them in front of the air-conditioners, he fired the man for deceiving customers. With that lesson, among others, he taught me that being a good person was more important than making money. He also wanted me to believe in something bigger and more powerful than my bank account.

My father encouraged me to pursue a career focused on helping people instead of making money. He believed wealthy people should share their good fortune. And, besides, he thought he'd made enough for his children to live out our lives in comfort. In the end, it was a promise he couldn't keep.

My First Business Trip

Desperate for my father's attention, I loved what he loved. I paid homage to Miracle Mart by going to work with him every Saturday. My job was to give away the free popcorn. I sat on a tall wooden stool and poured metal tins of pre-popped kernels into a whirring popcorn machine. Every five minutes, I scooped hot, salty kernels into small paper bags and passed them out to anyone who asked and some who didn't. I delighted in the surprised expression on shoppers' faces when they got something for free.

When I turned thirteen in 1961, my father took me to New York City. The trip was my baptism into a business world far removed from smiles and popcorn. He wanted to toughen me up. Like a faithful mutt, I tagged along at his heels while he wheeled and dealed in the backrooms of sweatshops. My clearest memory of the trip is how sore my feet were by the end. My second-clearest memory is of the backroom bribes. I slouched on the outskirts of conversations listening to fast-talking men tempt my father with free dinners at swanky restaurants, free front-row seats to sold-out shows, and free sexual favors from their so-called secretaries. His intent was to show me the dark side of business. After the trip, his advice to me was, "Don't take any shit; never owe a salesman a favor; and always get the best deal."

There's No Algebra in Accounting

That trip was the most time I ever spent one-on-one with my father. For the most part, he avoided me. He was afraid of me, afraid of the smell of failure. His fear wasn't without merit. I was a failure at the only thing that matters when you're a kid: school. If I'd grown up today, I would have been put in a special class for kids with learning disabilities. Instead, I was labeled an under-achiever, and most people just gave up on me. School is filled with subjects like spelling, grammar, and history, all requiring a knack for memorization and an eye for detail—two skills I sorely lacked. I could design a complex business plan, but I couldn't diagram a simple sentence. I was perpetually on the verge of flunking every class and was held back a year in junior high.

Luckily, I'm a math whiz. Like my father, I can calculate profits, returns, and risk ratios without putting pen to paper. As a child, numbers were my saving grace. I took solace in math. I've always solved elaborate equations in my head by working the math backward. My technique is unusual but effective.

The only time my math skills failed me was in high school—freshman algebra, to be exact. Looking back, I realized that the problem was that no one explained the theoretical concepts of algebra to me, which rendered my technique useless. My concerned parents hired an algebra tutor—a move that led to one of the biggest revelations of my life.

I was in the living room with my tutor while, unbeknown to me, my mother was eavesdropping from the kitchen. My tutor, a patient, well-meaning graduate student, explained how I would need algebra when I grew up to solve difficult business problems. I told her she was wrong. I could figure out what I needed to know without using a single algebraic formula. Assuming I was just being obstinate, she gave me a complicated business problem and challenged me to figure it out. I ticked off the correct answer. She got flustered. She lobbed harder and harder problems at me, and I came up with the correct answer every time (without using any algebra). She eventually gave up.

After she left, my mother told me she'd overhead the exchange. I braced myself for her wrath, but instead she said, "The last thing in the world you need is a math tutor. I think we should just leave you alone. You're going to be okay." It was an amazing thing for her to say. Until that point, I had considered myself a failure. No one had ever told me that I would be okay. With five simple words, my mother turned my life around.

But knowing I was going to be okay and getting through high school were two different things. I would have dropped out if my mother hadn't bribed me to finish. Here's the deal we struck: I told her I would do what it took to graduate if she gave me one day off a week. I could pick a day to play hooky, and she wouldn't bug me. On the other four days, I would go to school without a fight. She agreed. From that day on, every time I wanted a day off, she wrote a letter to the principal telling him I had a cold, and I spent the day looking for adventure. Without my mother's acceptance of my need to roam, I doubt I would have finished high school.

My Summer of Love

After graduating from high school in June 1967, I couldn't wait for college to start so I could escape from Ohio. I found out about the summer of love from an article in *Life* magazine. Sitting in my parents' living room, I read and reread the descriptions of San Francisco streets, then teeming with free love, marijuana, and psychedelics. Haight Street sounded as far from Akron, Ohio, as I could imagine. I had a trip in the works to visit my mother's father in Tacoma, Washington, so I hatched a plan to spend a few days in San Francisco to check out the hubbub for myself.

A few weeks later, I stepped off the bus and into the Summer of Love. Just like the photos in the magazine, people were singing, dancing, and partying in the streets. I saw hippies making love in the parks and police smoking marijuana. Like any other social movement, you couldn't just observe the Summer of Love; you had to participate. A natural at chess, I quickly settled into the dynamic chess scene in the Haight Street coffee houses. It didn't take long for me to meet people I never would have crossed paths with in Ohio—people like J.J.

I knew I was in trouble the minute J.J. sat down at my table. He was a tall, black man with sun-eclipsing hair and steel-toed boots. The hull of a hunting knife protruded from a sash at his hips. His first words to me were, "I'm going to kick your ass, white boy." And he did.

He mopped the chessboard with me and gave me a verbal lashing to boot. He played brilliantly, but he barely looked at the chessboard because he was so busy lecturing me. He accused me of being a racist, abusing poor people, instigating war in Vietnam, and ruining the environment. When he got up to leave, he spat, "You are just an arrogant, rich, white kid."

I responded with the only argument I could think of: "It's not my fault I've never met a black person who wasn't a maid. You're the one who is racist and prejudiced."

He sat back down. "All right, white boy, you say you want to learn a thing or two, but you better be serious. If you waste my time, I'm going to kick your ass."

J.J. was twenty-five when we met. He'd grown up in San Francisco and graduated from law school at the University of California at Berkeley. He taught me about chess, politics, revolution, racism, and Marxist economics. He was right: I had a lot to learn. He transformed an idealistic kid with good intentions into a nascent revolutionary. He knew everyone on Haight Street, from newspaper editors to poets. Over the next few weeks, he introduced me to dozens of people, including Bob Dylan. I was having so much fun, I called my parents and convinced them to let me stay in San Francisco for a month.

I've never seen as much heart and soul in my life as I saw on Haight Street in 1967. Everything was definite; everything was strong: the brightly colored clothes, the smell of incense and marijuana, and the lyrics of Joan Baez and Bob Dylan. Being yourself was the focus of life. I had the heart, and I learned the soul—how to project personality; how to be authentic; how to reach people; how to take the color, energy, and personality of the movement and channel it into something tangible.

I developed my business philosophy on Haight Street. To this day, I can't think of a better phrase than "gentle capitalism" to describe how I run my business life. It captures both my entrepreneurial spirit and the heart and soul of the hippie generation. It's no coincidence that many years later, I would settle and start businesses in San Francisco.

"I Think I Went to College"

Back in Akron, my parents considered my graduation from high school a miracle. I was ambivalent about higher education but eager to escape the Midwest and desperate to avoid the draft. I'd applied to schools in Colorado and California and at the last minute added Boston University to the list because it had a reputation for favoring high SAT scores over grade point averages. My SAT scores were terrific, but I'd graduated near the bottom of my class. As the spring wore on and the rejection letters accumulated, Boston University was the only school to accept me. Ironically, I'd applied to and was accepted by the business school. The choice was deliberate: I was more interested in poetry, but the business school was most likely to admit an underachieving high school senior with great test scores.

In Business, You Can't Accept the Status Quo

I found college far easier than high school, and being a good writer helped. I remember my first big assignment—a paper for Business 101, a survey class covering business theory under different economic systems. The grade from this assignment would equal one-third of my total grade in the course. The task was to explain why the industrial revolution wouldn't have happened without capitalism.

My gut reaction was to question the question. "Capitalism doesn't have a corner on economic growth," I thought. "Stalin, for one, accomplished a lot economically without capitalism." So I based my paper on the argument that no one could say whether capitalism was responsible for the industrial revolution. A week later, I handed in the paper thinking I'd probably get an F.

The next class period, the professor made a fuss over delivering our grades. He started off by saying the papers were terrible. Almost everybody scored a C, D, or F. But, he said, one person got an A. Then he read excerpts from the A paper. I was shocked to hear my words echo through the lecture hall. He finished by calling my name and asking me to come to the front of the auditorium.

"I'm giving you an A because you were the only student who questioned the question," he said. "In business, you can't accept the status quo. When something doesn't add up, you have to delve deeper in search of the answer."

Growing Up

In college, my social life also took a dramatic upturn. I'd been a loner for eighteen years, yet on my first day in the dorm, I fell into an unlikely friendship. I heard guitar music and went looking for the source. Four doors down, I stopped outside Jesse Brown's room. I walked in and said, "I betcha that's a Joan Baez song." From that moment on, our friendship was off and running. I soon found out that Jesse and a group of his high school friends had come to Boston from a closely knit Italian community in Rhode Island.

Over the course of the year, they adopted me as one of their own. They made me an "honorary Italian" and christened me Vinnie. I spent school holidays in Rhode Island with them and their families. I even tagged along to their high school reunion, where they introduced me as a member of the class.

We've remained close. One of the kids in the group was Anthony Russo, now a world-famous illustrator and my dearest friend. The late Jesse Brown, the guitar player, went on to become the road manager for the J. Geils Band. And Uncle Lou (so called because he was the only one among us who had nieces and nephews) is a successful talent agent in New York City.

They all came from working-class backgrounds, and I stuck out as the rich kid. They gave me a hard time about my privilege and how little I understood about life. But the teasing ended when they needed money. I believe in helping folks out, so I'd loan them money without any expectation of being paid back. Bankrolling my friends helped me feel less guilty about my privileged background and got them through college a little easier. My father referred to this as "Stuart's college scholarship fund" and good-naturedly gave me all the money I needed for my friends and me.

My new friends introduced me to Vermont. The summer of Woodstock we rented a house in Putney. Vermont felt like a magical kingdom. It was known for its nice people, clean environment, and low crime rates. I liked the fact that the state had a history of harboring intellectuals and poets because I considered myself on the verge of becoming both.

That summer my friends worked part time in town or on construction sites. I stayed home and wrote poetry, grocery shopped, and cooked. On weekends, we smoked marijuana and read Jack Kerouac and Kurt Vonnegut. I felt so at home in Vermont that I returned the following summer and stayed through the fall, dropping out of college before the start of my senior year. Although it would be several more years before I accepted my destiny of becoming a businessman like my father, I eventually chose Vermont as the backdrop for my first intentional business venture.

THE IMPORTANCE OF MENTORS

Entrepreneurship is not easy. There is no formal degree to earn or established ladder to climb. The best way to learn what it takes to be an entrepreneur is to find a mentor. Mentors can teach you the ins and outs of a business, and they can be role models. I was fortunate to have several role models in my family, but being born into a business family isn't the only way to secure a mentor. Consider these tips:

- Know you need a mentor. The more ambitious you are, the more help you'll require.
- Prioritize a mentoring relationship. Seek out a good mentor just as you'd seek out a great location, a favorable contract, or a business partner. Make a list of the qualities you'd like to find in a mentor, and don't settle for the first person who comes along.

- Show your appreciation. The best mentoring blossoms from a mutually beneficial relationship. What can you do to return the favor? Your contribution may be something as simple as cleaning your mentor's office or doing errands—look for a need your mentor has and fill it. For years, I repaid one of my mentors by acting as his family's personal movie adviser.

- Always be on the lookout for mentors; they may be in unlikely places. Join a professional organization. The more you circulate in your chosen field, the more likely you are to bump into potential mentors. But keep an open mind; anyone can be a mentor. Surprisingly, my psychotherapist became one of my most influential business mentors.

- Be specific. Don't approach a potential mentor with a vague cry for help. Be confident, and state your needs clearly. For example, don't say, "I want to be an entrepreneur. Tell me everything you know." Instead, focus your request—for example: "I want to be in the pharmacy business, and I know you are an expert in the field. Could you give me feedback on the viability of my business plan?"

- Do your homework. Before approaching a potential mentor, find out as much as you can about him or her. Question people who know this person. Familiarize yourself with his or her background. Your goal is for your potential mentor to see your due diligence as a sign of respect and an indication of your seriousness.

- Mentor others. People who go out of their way to help others attract people who want to help them. And sometimes the best way to repay a mentor is to pay it forward.

CHAPTER 2

Sex, Drugs, and the Business of Rock-and-Roll

Some went to business school;
I managed a rock band.
(Guess who had more fun?)

Sometimes a business can be started by accident. In 1972, I was a twenty-three-year-old aspiring poet. Launching a new business was the last thing on my mind, but that's exactly what happened. I unintentionally took the helm of a new company, and the experience was a wild ride of self-discovery. Although it would be another thirteen years before I fully embraced the idea of being an entrepreneur, my initial foray into the start-up world taught me a tremendous amount about what it takes to succeed.

An Unlikely Mentor

Two years earlier, I'd let my friends at Boston University convince me to become a musician. It was 1970, and everyone was either a musician or a wannabe. I knew I'd most likely fall into the second category because I had absolutely no talent. But no one else let that stop them, so who was I to go against the tide? When pressed by my friends to name my weapon, I chose the harmonica. I didn't have a natural affinity for the instrument, but it seemed like a good match because I had such a big mouth.

I liked playing the harmonica, but I wasn't very good. I had no musical ability. I needed a teacher. My college friends had befriended a man named James Montgomery who was a student at Boston University at the time and on his way to becoming a famous musician. He was playing harp for the Caldwell-Winfield Blues Band, a popular band in Boston.

The first time I met James, I asked him how much he'd charge me for a harmonica lesson. He stepped back and sized me up, then said, "You look like you're good for at least a six-pack."

"Hey, I'm good for at least two six-packs," I shot back, acting insulted.

"Deal."

And so I paid for my first harmonica lesson with two six-packs of Carling Black Label beer—James's favorite.

James gave me my lesson that afternoon on a park bench in Boston. Lucky for me, he was patient. I didn't have much of an ear for music, but he assured me I'd master the basics in no time. Slowly and carefully, he explained how to play the harmonica. Although I felt clumsy and tone deaf, James never lost his warmth, enthusiasm, and humor. I laughed so much it was hard to get my mouth around the instrument. By the end of the lesson, his confidence had rubbed off on me. I felt that I just might become a musician after all.

With the clarity of hindsight, I realize he gave me a one-man show that day in the park. He was an entertainer who never took insult at the size of his audience. (Years later, I saw him give one of the best performances of his career to three people in a ski lodge.) During that impromptu harmonica lesson, however, I never dreamed he'd be one of my most important business mentors.

The Accidental Entrepreneur

A couple of years later, I had just returned from Europe and was going to start driving a cab for Town Taxi and trying to be a writer when Uncle Lou, my friend from BU, asked me to help him start a rock-and-roll band management agency. Lou, who'd been booking neighborhood concerts in Boston that summer, had become friendly with the city's most popular local act, the James Montgomery Band. He and the band members had become fast friends, drinking and partying together after concerts. The guys in the band were drawn to Uncle Lou's down-to-earth manner and antiestablishment attitude. They trusted him. The band members also knew they were starting to become popular and needed business management, but they didn't want some greasy, slick manager. So they asked Uncle Lou to do the job.

A big fan of the band, Uncle Lou jumped at the chance to represent them. The next thing he did was ask if I would help. I considered his offer and figured, Why not? The job sounded more interesting than driving a cab, and I thought the ups and downs of managing a rock-and-roll band would be good fodder for a novel or screenplay. In hindsight, the job inspired me, but not as I'd expected.

Act Like You Know What You're Doing

My first few weeks on the job were like a sitcom. No sooner had I started working with Uncle Lou than he fell in love with a student at Smith College, ninety miles away in Northampton, Massachusetts. So before I knew it, I was running the company single-handedly. My first test came on the night of a concert in the Warren Towers dormitory at Boston University. Uncle Lou was out of town (of course) and asked me to cover for him. I hesitantly agreed. The problem was that most of the band members hadn't met me yet, so I wasn't sure how this was going to fly.

Sure enough, when I showed up, the security guards refused to let me near the stage door. The James Montgomery Band was very popular in Boston, especially among students. Hundreds of people were lining up outside the doors to get in, and I looked like just another kid trying to lie his way backstage. So there I was trying to convince the security guards I was the band's manager. Compounding my problem was the fact that although I was twenty-three, I looked fifteen. I sported a young Trotsky look: a rat's nest of hair, a scraggly beard, wire-rimmed glasses, and floppy clothing. Finally, one of the band members recognized me as Uncle Lou's sidekick, and the security guards grudgingly let me pass.

When I saw James backstage, we had an awkward moment. He grinned and asked me how my music was going. It was obvious he remembered me from our harmonica lesson in the park two years earlier but had no idea I was there to help Uncle Lou manage the band. Although he was obviously busy (he had a concert to play, after all), he stopped and gave me his full attention, almost as if he was going to launch into another music lesson right then and there. When I finally explained myself, we both had a good laugh and got on with the show.

Gaining entry into my own band's gigs was a reoccurring problem. It was easier to lie than to convince people I was the band's rightful manager. To get through security, I identified myself as a roadie, a friend of the band, or a band member's younger brother. Eventually I made up a fictitious manager, Harry Feinstein, and billed myself as his assistant. When someone asked me a question about the band, I'd say, "You should talk to the band's manager, Harry, but he's in Europe, so maybe I can help."

Working in the rock-and-roll business taught me the value of image and confidence. I learned how to be more effective in the business world by acting older and more confident than I felt. I had to project self-assurance to booking agents, promoters, the press, and, later, record company executives. Once I got into the habit of looking as if I knew what I was doing, people treated me differently—as if I were important. When people spoke, I'd look around for the person they were addressing. I thought they were talking to someone much older and more credible than me. I learned that if I acted older and more important than I felt, people took my word for it.

James showed me that feigning confidence was the best way to survive a bad situation. One night our drummer was late to a gig. Normally a band member running late was no big deal, but the club's owners were old-style gangsters and they were angry that my band wasn't on stage. To escape their wrath, I hid in the bathroom. Angelo, the club manager, was stomping around backstage bellowing, "Get your boys on stage! They're twenty minutes late!" I was cowering behind the door of the men's room when I heard James's voice come over the microphone: "Ladies and gentlemen, we have something very special for you tonight. We want to play some authentic Mississippi Delta blues, and therefore we'll play our first set without drums." This was James's way of making lemonade out of lemons. He acted as if leaving out the drums for an entire set was part of the plan. I slinked out of the bathroom, the band opened with an acoustic set, and the audience went wild.

Be Authentic, and They Will Come

As I'd experienced that day in the park with my harmonica, James had a way of making everyone feel special. His charisma and humor drew people to him, even in an auditorium with thousands of people. By the end of his show, he'd have the audience on their feet, dancing and singing three-part harmonies. Even the police, most of whom hated hippies and "young people's" music, ended up tapping their toes to the James Montgomery Band, repeating his jokes to their buddies, and joining James for a beer after the show. Everyone who met him fell under his spell. I bet today, thirty years later, if you tracked down people who were at those concerts, they'd remember James.

James was also successful because of his authenticity. In Boston, his band was known as "the band of the people." You could count on him to be at the forefront of a civil rights demonstration or an antiwar protest. For James, making money was secondary to standing up for his beliefs. He insisted I book the band for so many free shows at benefits and prisons that we regularly went for weeks making no money at all. He was especially kind to less fortunate musicians. He always asked me to help his many struggling-musician friends. I did what I could, offering free career advice, a few connections, and occasionally a gig. James always thought we should do more.

But authenticity alone isn't enough to succeed in show business. In fact, show business is one of the most cutthroat businesses in the world. It's full of sharks ready to take advantage of musicians who are more focused on their music than the fine print in their contracts. If you want to succeed in the music business, you need to be business savvy—or hire someone who is. But you also need to be authentic because the greatest contract in the world is worthless without an excited audience filling the venue.

James Montgomery's authenticity, along with his sincere caring for his audience and, more important for the world around him, his heart and soul, was the secret to his band's success. In that way, he was my teacher and a role model for my future career as a heart-and-soul entrepreneur.

Do Whatever It Takes—and Don't Count the Hours

There I was, all of twenty-three years old and managing a hot
rock-and-roll band. At that time, the James Montgomery Band
was arguably one of the most successful unrecorded bands in
history in the United States. We headlined concerts, sold thousands of tickets, and pocketed thousands of dollars a night.

Although we were a huge success, I was constantly reminded
that we were also just a bunch of kids, and more often than not,
I had to be the parent. During office hours, I had a phone stuck
to each ear booking gigs, promoting the band, and managing the
roadies. By 5:00 P.M., when other people were leaving work, I was
only halfway through my day. Knowing the band was still sleeping off last night's hangovers, I'd make the rounds of their apart-
ments and wake them up for that night's gig. Like a mother
rounding up her charges, I made sure everybody got up, ate, and
made it to the show on time. Once the band was accounted for, I
had to shift gears again to manage the concert. My days never
ended before midnight. Then I'd get up the next morning and
do it all over again.

If you start any business counting the hours you work or lim-
iting the tasks you're willing to shoulder, your business will fail.
You're better off taking a job with a corporation and heading for
a cubicle. Entrepreneurs love their companies and will do whatever it takes for the company to succeed. In Chapter Four, you'll
meet a pioneer of the natural foods business who spent weekends stocking the shelves of his stores. My business was the
James Montgomery Band, and I knew that waking and feeding
bleary-eyed musicians was as important to the success of that
business as cutting deals with concert promoters.

Make Sure All Employees Share Your Enthusiasm

Although the musicians are in the limelight, a rock-and-roll band is like any business—it needs a talented and enthusiastic support staff. At live gigs, that support staff is the diverse crew of technicians, drivers, carpenters, and others who transport, build, and operate the stage and equipment. I found managing the tough blue-collar roadies, as they are known, as much of a challenge as managing the musicians.

One human resource lesson I learned was the importance of starting new employees off on the right foot. The roadie who managed our equipment had a bad attitude: he griped all the time and was so unpleasant to be around that no one wanted to work with him. But instead of firing him, I gave him the responsibility of training a new employee. The cranky roadie quickly passed his bad attitude on to the new guy, so although the first roadie eventually quit, the new guy's attitude was tarnished, and we never rid ourselves of the problem. I kept that lesson in mind when I opened the second of my chain of video stores, Empire Video. When it was time to select who would train the new employees, I made a conscious effort to choose employees who were enthusiastic about both their jobs and the company as a whole. Sure enough, the good vibe was passed on from one employee to the next, and Empire's second store had a great staff that reflected the good vibe of the original location.

Seek Out Your Customers, and Listen to What They Say

Bullshit is inevitable in any line of work, but it's rampant in show business. I tried to extract constructive feedback from people but was usually unsuccessful. Getting positive feedback was a snap. People naturally told me the band was wonderful but were hesitant to elaborate on what they didn't like. After every concert, people would gush to me about how the band was the best they'd ever heard, how they played the best music, came up with the best melodies, had the best energy, and on and on. But platitudes aren't helpful when you're trying to develop a business.

I knew the band was pleasing the crowds most of the time, but I also knew some of the concerts were stinkers. Determined to get the truth about what we were doing wrong, I started picking up hitchhikers while driving around Boston. Without telling them who I was or what I did for a living, I'd ask them questions about their taste in music. Luckily, the James Montgomery Band was so popular that half the people I picked up knew about the band, and many had been to a recent concert. So I'd ask them for their opinions on the band, the music, and the latest concert they had attended. I got some of my best feedback that way; hitchhikers were totally honest. They didn't hesitate to tell me when the drums were too loud, when James was too drunk to sing coherently, or when the bass solo was too long. These spontaneous "focus groups" became my favorite market research tool.

One mistake business owners make is thinking they know best. They think they know what their customers want or like. I may have been the manager of a successful band, but the truth is that I had horrible taste in music. Just before I entered the music business, I was at the Boston Tea Party, a local rock club, when the famous British guitar player Jeff Beck made his American debut with his new band. Jeff was a great guitar player but had a lousy voice, so he'd hired a singer. I thought the new singer had an equally awful voice. He sang like he had a frog stuck in his throat. Getting up to leave, I turned to my friend and said, "Boy, this guy's terrible; he's never going to make it." The singer's name was Rod Stewart.

I had a similar experience with Aerosmith. The band was from Boston and had opened for James Montgomery. At one point, they expressed interest in my managing them, but I didn't pursue it. When people asked me why, I told them, "Those guys are going nowhere. They are just a bad imitation of the Rolling Stones."

Ouch.

Eventually I got smart enough to ignore my taste in music. Instead I stuffed cotton in my ears, sat on the stage, and watched the audience. A band's success can be predicted by the audience's reaction. By focusing my attention on the audience, I was able to tell if the band was making a strong impression. I could tell if the audience members would go home and talk up the music to their friends and if they would pony up if we raised our ticket prices. Learning how to focus on my customers' tastes rather than my own was an important, early business lesson that has served me well.

Any successful businessperson knows you have to do whatever it takes to get objective market research. Just spouting off about what you think the market wants or needs isn't good enough. Neither is listening to yes people who just tell you what you want to hear. In my case, getting objective market research meant picking up long-haired, opinionated hitchhikers. And it worked.

It's All About Brand, Baby

Marketing comes as naturally to me as breathing, but attention to detail does not. That's why the rock-and-roll business proved to be a great business for me. We had a saying, "That's close enough for rock-and-roll," meaning the details weren't important. In show business, details take a backseat to image. In the end, the big picture was all that mattered, and image was more important than reality.

So when a young reporter from a major newspaper approached me about writing a feature story about the band, I couldn't believe our good fortune. Even as an accidental entrepreneur, I knew the value of great press.

Once the reporter got his editor's okay to travel with the band to do his "research," I knew it was in our best interest to make him happy, so I asked the boys to show him a good time. Like a lot of other young men, he was into drugs, sex, and rock-and-roll, especially the sex. He'd been traveling with the band for two months when his editors started bugging him to turn in his story. He had the chutzpah to tell them that it was such a complex assignment he needed another two months. In truth, he was having so much fun he didn't want to go home. Without a doubt, this guy had the time of his life. In the end, he wrote a raving front-page story. As a result, the band's popularity skyrocketed, my phone rang off the hook, and our fees doubled.

It didn't take long to secure record contracts and start recording albums. The James Montgomery Band went on to open for many famous musicians, most often the Allman Brothers, Bonnie Raitt, Steve Miller, and Edgar Winter.

Learn About Supply and Demand (Heart and Soul Aren't Enough)

What most artists don't understand is that the business world runs on math, meaning that people aren't rewarded on talent alone. Most musicians are poorly paid because the supply of musical talent is much greater than the demand. Financial rewards go to musicians who draw customers into a club. Club owners and concert promoters don't care if a musician is good; they just want to make money. Musicians who draw big audiences command higher fees because they are assigned a higher economic value in the marketplace.

Working under this rule, the James Montgomery Band made plenty of money. We all had a salary, a place to live, and food in our bellies, which is more than most other musicians at the time. When other artists asked me to do the same for them, I'd tell them, "I'd love to, but it's not that easy. James is a success because he's a great entertainer, not because of me."

Most often, they'd respond, "What do you mean? I'm a great musician too."

So I'd say, "That's really cool. I'm a musician-wannabe, and I'm jealous of your talent, but being a musician and making a living as one are two different things. If you want to earn a living, you must get paid by someone who values your services."

The question entertainers need to ask themselves is not, Are we talented? but, Do we have drawing power?

James also taught me about using supply and demand to the band's advantage. He and his guitar player, Larry, studied the way other successful bands, like the J. Geils Band, benefited from keeping their concerts in short supply. We avoided overplaying large markets like Boston. That way, when we did schedule a show, it was a special event, and people were willing to pay a premium. With the free time, we focused on expanding into new territory by playing in smaller cities. We quickly conquered new markets because the band was such a great live act. Once we played a new venue, word spread fast. For instance, only three people came to see us play our first night in ski country, but by the end of the week, the club was packed.

You Need the Complete Package

By 1973 the James Montgomery Band was filling venues throughout New England and opening for major bands and singers. The next step for an up-and-coming band was to start recording, hitting the charts, and eventually becoming nationally and internationally known. But the band had reached its peak. Their concerts were lively musical parties, but becoming a major musical success takes more than a dynamic stage performance. They were fantastic live, but their voices were weak and their lyrics mediocre. Without the complete package, they couldn't succeed in the recording studio and therefore couldn't find their footing on a national level.

The same concept applies to any other business. The mission of a natural food store such as Whole Foods Market is to provide healthy food. But all the components of a quality grocery store must be in place to keep customers coming back; for example, the stores need to be clean and the shelves stocked. Being authentic, having heart and soul, and being driven by the best of intentions aren't good enough to succeed in business.

Know When to Leave the Business—No Matter What Your Age

Eventually the combination of eighteen-hour days, the stress of keeping the guys in line, and the heartbreak of the band's slow downhill slide all became too much. After three years of managing the James Montgomery Band, I was physically and emotionally exhausted. To reach the next tier of success, the band needed to make the transition from playing live shows to selling records, and I knew it was never going to happen. The James Montgomery Band was a great live act, but its charisma didn't translate to recordings.

I could have jumped ship and gone to work for another band. Several record company executives had approached me with offers, but taking one would have meant turning my back on my friends. Managing a band is an all-or-nothing job: you're either behind a band 100 percent or you drop it. There is no middle ground.

Unable to abandon James, I left the music business at age twenty-five and retired. This was the start of a work pattern I continued all the way up to age fifty-seven: busting my butt for two or three years, burning out, and following up with a quiet period where I rest up for my next big adventure. Some people are long-distance runners; I'm a sprinter.

In hindsight, I was a pretty good manager. My natural marketing talent combined with caring about the people in the band and wanting the best for them coalesced into a successful ride for all of us.

One day twelve years later, I was in a blues club in Harvard Square. I glanced at the monitors downstairs where I was sitting. They showed who was on stage upstairs. I couldn't believe how well the band's leader imitated James Montgomery. After dinner, I wandered upstairs to see this guy for myself. Not only was the musician doing a perfect imitation of James; it was James! He was so happy to see me that he worked my name, Stu, into every song for the rest of the night. He even played an embarrassing song he'd written during our time together, called "Do the Stu." Years after that first harmonica lesson, he was still teaching me about show biz and about heart and soul.

DESIGN YOUR BUSINESS TO ATTRACT GOOD PRESS

When creating a new business, design it to attract publicity from the beginning. Think about your business idea from a public relations standpoint. Can the business get good press? Is there a story? Is it topical? Is the business something people will want to read about? One of the most important PR decisions is your business's name and tagline. Before christening your business, ask yourself, Does the name get people's attention? Does it have positive associations? Does it sound authentic? Can the name help get us good press? Don't be afraid to choose a name that some people hate. You want something a little edgy because people respect a businessperson who takes risks. If nine out of ten people love the name, you're probably onto something. Some people had negative reactions to the word *elephant.* Some associated the name with being overweight and therefore unhealthy. Others were turned off because the elephant is a symbol of the Republican party. But neither group dissuaded me. I went ahead and named my latest company Elephant Pharmacy. I thought the name was fun and attention grabbing and wasn't bothered by the minority of people who didn't like it. Besides, if a business's name elicits strong reactions, good or bad, from people, it's more likely to draw attention.

CHAPTER 3

Bankruptcy at Home

*How I tried and failed to save
my father's business.*

Leaving the rock-and-roll business made me come face to face with the power of my addiction. For three years, I'd been on a continuous high—not on drugs, but on adrenaline. The music, the gigs, and the travel added up to a nonstop thrill. Now, without the energy of the band around me, I couldn't get a fix. I felt as if I'd been turned inside out. With hindsight, I see that managing musicians was a job that fit my personality to a tee. In the music business, everyone is colorful, so no one cared about my quirks. Managing the band kept my hyperactive, multitasking brain firing on all cylinders day in and day out.

Plus, I believed in James Montgomery and what he was doing. His integrity and desire to give back to both his fans and his community fed my need to be a part of something bigger than myself. But at the time, I couldn't see the synergy. Managing the band felt like being a businessman, and I wanted to be a writer. On some level, I believed I was edging closer to my father than felt comfortable. So I quit the band to pursue my dream of writing poetry.

Unmoored, I did what so many other music industry dropouts do: moved to northern California. I settled in Lagunitas, a bucolic town in Marin County, twenty miles north of San Francisco. For the next eighteen months, I made a go at being a full-time writer. I paced; I soul-searched; I sat on the beach with nothing but my journal for company; I wrote for days on end; I studied the craft of writing; I filled dozens of spiral-bound notebooks with mediocre short stories; I traveled to writers' conferences.

But deep down it wasn't working. When a creative writing teacher told me I lacked the patience to be a professional writer, I knew he was right. I was going through the motions, but I didn't have the talent to back it up. I woke up, as if from a dream, and looked around. That's when I realized I had no job and few friends in California. Without the dream of becoming a writer, I was more lost than ever before. Tired of being alone, I returned to Boston.

Politics and Rock-and-Roll Don't Mix

Back in Boston, I was captivated by the upcoming 1976 presidential campaign. A media junkie, I knew the issues inside and out. I'd followed the careers of the liberal candidates and was enamored with Morris Udall, a democratic congressman from Arizona. His strong stance on environmental issues rang true to me. He seemed authentic, like someone I would like to have as a friend. Since I had time on my hands, I volunteered for his presidential campaign. Over the next six months, I was promoted and became one of four paid staff members in Massachusetts. I coordinated media events as well as recruited and organized student volunteers in more than forty New England colleges. I considered myself perfect for the job. Politics felt like rock-and-roll— all big egos, brand recognition, and stage performances.

I got Udall some good press, but the higher-ups hated me. A clique of Yale-educated lawyers, they were uncomfortable with my rock-and-roll background and resented my habit of comparing politics to the music business. They considered the two things night and day: rock-and-roll was all drugs and sex, while politics was wrapped in civic duty and patriotism. I was effective on the campaign trail, but I knew it wouldn't last. As the staff grew and the campaign caught on, I felt increasingly out of place. My high-energy, all-or-nothing persona clashed with the growing hierarchy. I read the writing on the wall and left just as the campaign was getting off the ground. Again, I found myself out in the cold.

Return of a Native Son

Meanwhile, back in Akron, the discount retail industry had turned into a tough market. In the nine years since I had left, the local business atmosphere had changed dramatically. When Wal-Mart and Kmart blew into town with price guns blazing, Miracle Mart took a big hit. The national chains, with their enormous advertising budgets and international purchasing power, easily overpowered my family's best efforts.

My father, now sixty years old, faced the biggest crisis of his life. He'd assumed staggering amounts of debt, and the company was gasping for air. My mother feared for his health. I despised Ohio and had spent my life avoiding a career in the retail industry, but I was the only family member with an aptitude for business who was old enough to help. I did the only thing I could do: moved home and took over operations at Miracle Mart.

Miracle Mart Needed a Miracle

The year was 1976. Miracle Mart had nine stores, four hundred employees, and a handful of warehouses scattered throughout northern Ohio. I spent my first week on the job touring every store, office, and warehouse. I was disheartened by what I saw. Once a state-of-the-art enterprise, the company was a shell of its former self. What I remembered as bright, clean, and appealing stores were dirty, outdated, and depressing. The management, once enthusiastic and customer friendly, was corrupt and in disarray. The robust company of my childhood was gone.

Over the next year and a half, I tried my best to resuscitate the dying company. I began by replacing most of the store managers. Next, I cut costs by eliminating costly services, like the fresh meat departments. Finally, I found creative ways to use our real estate. For instance, I turned a huge vacant store in Warren, Ohio, into a flea market.

That decision to turn Miracle Mart's empty warehouses into flea markets was the highlight of my Ohio experience. I love marketplaces where customers and sellers come face-to-face. To guarantee our flea market would have the best goods around, I traveled to every farmer's market in the region; picked out the vendors with the highest-quality meats, cheeses, and baked goods; and convinced them to come sell their wares at our market. I wouldn't take no for an answer. When the Amish bakers told me they couldn't come because they didn't drive, I offered to pick them up myself. Once I'd persuaded the vendors to show up, I organized a huge promotion to kick off the market's opening day, and it was a resounding success. Ironically, the Warren Indoor Flea Market outlived Miracle Mart by at least ten years.

Looking back, I realize that my efforts were well intentioned, but I wasn't the guy to save my father's company. I was too young and had too little experience. Miracle Mart needed an operations expert, a nuts-and-bolts guy who knew how to streamline the company and make its systems efficient. At the end of the day, operations weren't my bag. I was a creative marketing guy with big ideas—not to mention, I was still suffering from my rock-and-roll hangover. I had a hard time wrapping my head around this traditional business in the heartland. As hard as I tried, I couldn't save my family's business, but I could save their reputation.

Going Broke

Finally, the situation became desperate: Miracle Mart was broke, and we declared bankruptcy. The banks' lawyers and bankruptcy liquidators wanted to take over. We knew they wouldn't do a good job liquidating the company and were worried our creditors would not be paid. My family takes tremendous pride in repaying its debts.

A meeting was scheduled between my family and representatives from the two banks to which we were most in debt. They were determined to handle the liquidation on their own, but we feared they would bungle the details of leasing the stores, selling off the remaining inventory, and smoothing things over with the employees. The night before the meeting, I couldn't sleep. Having been an amateur poker player, I knew we had to bluff. So I hatched a plan.

The next morning, I drove to the stores, collected all the keys, and put them on a huge ring. Then I drove to the bank to meet my family and the lawyers. Ten minutes into the meeting, I produced the fistful of keys and dangled it in front of the banks' lawyers.

"You guys don't know anything about our customers, our employees, or our merchandise," I said, "but if you want to run the bankruptcy, fine. It's all yours. We're leaving town because we don't want to be blamed for the mess you'll make."

I threw the keys down on the desk and walked out with my family in tow.

I was bluffing, but the banks' representatives didn't know better. Later that day, they caved. They agreed to let us control the process under the supervision of a bankruptcy court. It was the best possible outcome for us.

A Happy Ending to a Sad Story

We had an incredibly successful bankruptcy sale. Knowing a going-out-of-business sale was inevitable, we'd spent months stocking up on seconds, irregulars, and odd lots that would sell quickly. We'd also worked to free ourselves of our real estate obligations by subleasing our stores. With the landlords assuaged, cash from the sale went straight to paying our debt.

In the end, we paid our creditors eighty-five cents on the dollar. They were delighted, and the banks' lawyers told me it was the most successful going-out-of-business sale they'd ever seen. A smooth ending to Miracle Mart's saga was my proudest moment in Ohio. My father retired to Arizona, and I was free to do as I pleased.

Grown Up at Last

On my twelve-hour drive back to Boston, I had ample time to reflect on what I'd learned since retiring from the rock-and-roll business. Mostly I'd discovered what I didn't want to do. I didn't fit into politics. I didn't enjoy mainstream retailing. I didn't like retirement. I didn't make it as a writer. As I surveyed my options, a thunderbolt hit me: I wasn't a rich kid anymore. I'd grown up with everything money could buy. Now my father had narrowly escaped from Miracle Mart with just enough money for his retirement.

Questions filled my head: What if I never have a career? What if I die poor and useless? What if I'm not good at anything? Somewhere in eastern Ohio, the panic subsided and something else crept in: excitement. When I stepped out of the car in Boston, I jumped up and down with giddiness. I didn't realize how much my father's money had weighed me down until it was gone. I felt free to find myself, to be my own man. For the first time in my life, I had to take care of myself. I'd spent my life feeling dysfunctional because I was shackled to my father and his money. I was out of the shadow of my father and the family business. I finally felt grown up, and it felt good.

CHAPTER 4

Helping to Invent Whole Foods

Battles with my mentor made me wiser, confident, and determined never to work for anybody again.

I could have been a real estate mogul. I could have been the Donald Trump of Boston (without the bankruptcies). I could have bought and sold land, developed properties, and built shiny skyscrapers filled with the offices of financial companies willing to pay outrageous amounts for each square foot. In 1978, I had everything in place for a career in commercial real estate. I had the contacts. I had the certificate. I was on my way. But I knew I wanted to make my millions in another field.

There were two things wrong with real estate: (1) it was boring, and (2) I wanted to work in an industry with heart and soul. Before I tell you how I found my heart-and-soul business at a grocery chain called Bread & Circus, where I learned more about being a successful entrepreneur and business leader than anywhere else, let me first tell you about my unhappy but necessary detour into what I consider the barren wasteland of big-time real estate.

Out of Defeat, a Plan for Success

Business is a strange world; it can be both serendipitous and exacting. After the bankruptcy of my father's business, I knew it was time to get serious about my future. I was twenty-eight years old, and I'd just returned to Boston after spending a year and a half helping my father try to save Miracle Mart. Although we couldn't salvage the company, we did pay off most of his debt by selling off the retail stores. In the process, I got a crash course in commercial real estate. Slowly I realized this was an area I could leverage into a high-level business career. During those sad days when we were painfully signing away what was left of my father's company, I was piecing together in my mind the steps I could take to further my career. Out of the defeat in Akron came a plan for success—and it worked.

Step One: Learning a Valuable Skill

Real estate decisions can make or break any retail business. The old saw about location, location, location is no joke. In the world of retail leasing, millions of dollars are at stake. Retail leasing is the retail part of commercial real estate. Essentially your job is to help stores find the best locations. You get paid a commission for each successful search. Because of the importance of retail leasing to the success of a store, top executives value people who are experts in this field, and there aren't many of them. By the time I got into the business, there were perhaps a dozen people making a living doing retail leasing in and around Boston.

As I helped my father and discovered the business value of real estate know-how, it dawned on me that commercial real estate could be my ticket into the upper echelon of business. Back in Boston, I signed up for real estate courses, prepared for my broker's license, and began networking. The owner of a small company specializing in retail leasing taught one of my classes. When I got my license, he hired me, and my career as a commercial real estate agent was off and running.

Once my retail leasing career at the AD Hillyer Company, the small real estate firm I worked for, was in full swing, I was ready to move to the next phase of my plan. I had a valuable skill and was meeting and working with the top management of growing local companies, a successful first step. But I never intended to be a hired hand for just any company. I was ready to focus on working with companies I believed in. Like many other lucrative fields, real estate is full of bloodthirsty people who'd rather get rich quick than save the world. Sure, I had my real estate license, but I wasn't like other brokers. I was a hippie vegetarian who rode his bike to work. I was a champion of the underdog. I could never work for companies like fast food chains that poison kids with junk food. What I wanted was to work for a feel-good, do-good business like my local grocery store: Bread & Circus.

Step Two: Connecting with a Heart-and-Soul Business

Bread & Circus exemplified my idea of a heart-and-soul business. Whereas conventional grocery stores stocked anything that turned a profit, from cigarettes to Spam, Bread & Circus took a different approach. The company carried organic foods, natural personal care products, and chemical-free cleaners. In essence, it elevated customer health above the lure of a quick dime. Today hundreds of health food businesses, including Whole Foods, which would buy Bread & Circus in 1994, do business this way. But in the 1970s for a grocery store to refuse to carry anything laced with chemicals and preservatives was a radical concept. Sometimes, though, radical new concepts strike a chord with the public.

I shopped religiously at my neighborhood Bread & Circus and heard nothing but good things about its owner, Anthony Harnett. A businessman with a penchant for healthy eating, Anthony bought the original Bread & Circus store in Brookline, Massachusetts, in 1975. The combination of his attention to detail, ability to crunch numbers, and devotion to health made him a force in the industry. Soon Bread & Circus was the largest natural food retailer in the Northeast.

Convinced we'd have a lot in common, I set out to meet Anthony. I started by phoning his office. I called daily for a month, but he never returned my messages. I'm not usually a pest, but this was important, and I wasn't about to give up, so I sweet-talked his secretary into telling me how I might improve my chances of getting his attention. She divulged that he could often be found late in the afternoons stocking shelves at the store. Thinking it was just another wild goose chase, I went to the store the next afternoon. Sure enough, he was in the back aisle slapping price tags on bags of granola.

I walked up, introduced myself, and stuck out my hand. After a guarded handshake, Anthony politely made it clear that he was too busy to chat with salesmen. Although discouraged, I didn't give up. Whenever I had a free afternoon, I'd drop by and talk to him while he worked. My goal was twofold: to convince him of my real estate prowess and to impress on him my personal devotion to a healthy lifestyle. At first, his response to my diatribes consisted of the occasional nod. But eventually I got the feeling he was really listening. The day he tossed me an apron and told me to help him out while we talked real estate is the day I knew I'd made it.

Anthony grew to trust that I knew a thing or two about the city's commercial real estate and eventually let me take a stab at finding his next store. After scouring the surrounding neighborhoods for prime real estate, I found a scruffy storefront on Prospect Street in Cambridge, Massachusetts. The reason this location was such an untapped resource was that it was in a seedy urban neighborhood but it had great parking, a rarity in Cambridge, and it was strategically located by several up-and-coming neighborhoods filled with potential customers. The Prospect Street store opened in 1979 and went on to become the highest-volume natural foods store in the nation. Later Anthony bought the building, and it became an important asset for him when financing his fast-growing company. I'm not bragging when I say that the location for the Prospect Street store put Anthony on the map and was instrumental in his future success. As of the writing of this book, the store still stands.

Afterward Anthony and I developed a close working relationship. I stayed in real estate for another year or so, but more and more I was focusing on Bread & Circus. I loved the company. I had eaten natural foods for years and was a firm believer in brown rice and tofu as the elixir of life. This was something I had a real passion for. A lot of the companies I did real estate work for weren't very interesting. They were mostly clothing retailers—people who didn't care about the big picture. They weren't doing harm, but they weren't doing good for the world either. My passion for Bread & Circus kept growing. Finally, after my success with the Prospect Street store, Anthony brought me onto the payroll.

Retailing 101

Bread & Circus was too small to have a dedicated real estate guru on staff, so I was hired as the company's real estate hunter, human resource director, and marketing expert. The job sounds like a mishmash, but having multiple job titles at a small business isn't unusual. You've got to make the most of the few people you can afford to hire. Juggling three positions was a challenge, but it gave me the opportunity to learn several areas of the business at once—something that came in handy when I founded my own business years later.

I had a lot to learn about the natural foods business, so Anthony gave me an apron and put me to work in the store for six weeks. I spent the first three weeks learning the ins and outs of the grocery department. Then I spent a week each in the produce, dairy, and supplement departments. The experience gave me a thorough training in all aspects of the store's basic operations—preparation that paid off later. As the human resource director, for example, I was hiring for jobs I'd done myself. How many other people can say they've done every job at a particular company?

In the two years I spent working for Bread & Circus, I learned the detailed operational demands of retailing. Because of Anthony Harnett's hard-driving personality and incredible business acumen, I also learned firsthand what it takes to be a successful leader. And, finally, I learned something about myself: that my best shot at success was to be my own boss.

My first real learning at Bread & Circus was in human resources. As the human resource director, I quickly discovered that feel-good businesses attract feel-good employees, who are not necessarily hard working. It didn't take me long to realize most of the job applicants needed a reality check.

Human Resources: Lazy New Agers Need Not Apply

My biggest accomplishments at Bread & Circus were in human resources. As the human resource manager, I was in charge of hiring for all four store locations. When I arrived, the company was hemorrhaging money because it couldn't hire and train enough qualified managers for its fast-growing stores.

Finding good people wasn't easy. Any new business concept has a hiring disadvantage because there is little overlap with other companies in terms of job skills and corporate culture. For instance, when we hired people from the local supermarkets, their skills looked great on paper, but their straitlaced personalities often clashed with the store's new age culture. Yet when I hired people who were drawn to the alternative atmosphere, they often lacked either the skills or the work ethic to make a great employee.

Here are some of the lessons I learned as human resources director:

Make snap decisions with confidence. I learned how to size people up quickly and make snap decisions with confidence. Some days I fielded more than a hundred phone calls from job seekers. If I gave everyone the benefit of the doubt, I'd make it through only three or four of the dozens of interviews I often needed to complete in one day. In the name of efficiency, I had to get to know people fast and make split-second decisions about whether to recommend them for hiring. Hiring people who would stick around was important; most of our job descriptions were deceptively complicated and took up to three months to master.

Watch out for enthusiasts without experience; they are often better customers than workers. At the time of my hiring craze, Ronald Reagan was cutting federal job spending for teachers and social workers. As a result, dozens of my customers came to me asking for work. I hired them thinking they would be model employees. After all, they were intelligent people with college degrees who knew the difference between tempe and seitan, and they loved the store. But my hiring shortcut backfired: within a few weeks, it became clear that most of my new employees would rather stand around debating the pros and cons of the oil embargo than roll up their shirtsleeves and get to work. What the customers didn't know about the store is that natural or not, groceries are a tonnage business. Tons of product come in the back door to be prepped, packaged, and shipped out the front door. It's a physically demanding, heavy-volume business.

Don't trust people to know if they'd like a particular job. Enthusiasm alone isn't enough. If a job similar to the one you are filling isn't listed on an applicant's résumé, tread carefully. People who haven't held similar positions in the past might not know enough about themselves to realize they won't be happy. Not everyone I hired during those early months left with their tails between their legs. Those who flourished often had had prior experience in restaurants and supermarkets and weren't afraid of physical labor.

Always look for potential managers. Since we wanted to build the company quickly, Anthony and I knew virtually every new employee needed to have management potential. In many ways, hiring, training, and motivating store managers is at the heart of retailing, especially for a store like Whole Foods or Elephant Pharmacy where there are lots of job descriptions and dozens of decisions to be made at the store level.

Finding good store managers was my biggest challenge. Store managers literally run the show. They hire, fire, motivate, and train the staff. They must stay on top of forty different job descriptions, many with health and safety risks. It's their responsibility to make sure everyone from the cashiers to the deli workers are well trained.

Managing a large store is almost as demanding as having your own business. It's difficult to find and hard to assimilate these kinds of entrepreneurial-minded people into a company because they'd often rather be their own boss. But you keep going after good people because talented store managers mean the company has a much better shot at success.

Operations: Don't Kill Your Customers (and Other Details)

The complexity of the business made hiring the right people a challenge. A store like Bread & Circus is one of the most difficult retail businesses to run and manage operationally. For instance, there were about forty different job descriptions in a Bread & Circus: cashier, bagger, front-end manager, meat manager, meat cutter, produce manager, produce worker, vitamin manager, and vitamin worker, to name just a few. By comparison, a clothing retailer like the Gap may have only three job descriptions in their stores: manager, assistant manager, and sales clerk.

Although the job descriptions of a grocery store sound straightforward, every person in every job must be carefully trained. Each store has six departments of perishables that need weekly inventories and careful management. In all food situations, you need clean, conscientious employees. This is even more important for natural foods stores because, unlike mainstream grocery stores, they don't use preservatives. Keeping food fresh is a constant worry. A poorly trained employee could kill a customer by allowing spoiled food to remain on the shelf.

In addition to the safety concerns, the minutia involved in running a natural foods store like Bread & Circus is mind-boggling. For example, we had an employee who did nothing for weeks at a time but pick through pints of strawberries and discard spoiled berries. Most supermarkets routinely sell containers of strawberries with moldy, crushed berries at the bottom. People who shop at conventional grocery stores expect to throw away a third of their strawberries. But at Bread & Circus, selling strawberries with a layer of rotting fruit at the bottom wasn't how we did business. And that level of detail wasn't restricted to the produce section; every department in the store was run with similar attentiveness.

Leadership: It Takes a Tough Man to Run a Natural Foods Store

I have met and befriended many CEOs and other business and nonbusiness leaders, but Anthony Harnett will always be my most important business mentor. As the human resource director at Bread & Circus, I quickly learned that our best customers made our worst employees. A natural foods store on the surface seems to be a laid-back affair. It isn't. Behind the scenes, a natural foods grocery needs a tough, demanding culture because everything has to be right. Without quality, the business will fail.

That is why Anthony Harnett was the perfect CEO for Bread & Circus. He was tough, opinionated, and intimidating and as far from a laid-back hippie as anyone could be. Anthony's character was forged in Ireland. He grew up poor. His mother died when he was young. Sometimes there wasn't food on the table. He is the only person I've ever known who grew up going to bed hungry. Anthony struggled in ways most Americans can't imagine.

In his late teens, Anthony moved to England because there were no jobs in Ireland. He cut his teeth in retailing at the famed department store Harrods, where he was accepted into the management trainee program.

Anthony was drawn to natural foods early in life. He adopted a macrobiotic diet in his early twenties. His diet was like a religion for him and led him to the natural foods business. He was the only entrepreneur in the industry who wasn't a hippie, and given the business's complexity, his straitlaced persona worked to his benefit and helped him become a major player.

When I was a kid, television commercials featured Frank Perdue, owner of the world's largest chicken company, saying: "It takes a tough man to make a tender bird." That's true of natural food stores as well. It takes a tough man to make a good natural food store.

Here are the key business lessons I learned from Anthony Harnett.

Own Your Mistakes; Then Keep Moving

One of the most important business lessons I took away from Anthony's tutelage was to let go of my mistakes. At one point, I hired a supermarket manager from a headhunter in Rhode Island. I was skeptical of the person's abilities, but the headhunter guaranteed me my money back if I wasn't happy, so I took a chance on the guy. I spent three months trying to make the situation work, but he didn't fit our culture. Neither the employees nor the customers liked him. Finally, right before our guarantee was scheduled to run out, we fired him. When I contacted the headhunter, he'd moved to a different state, and basically said, "F*** you." Going after him legally didn't make much sense because the legal fees would have cost us more than the money he owed us. Thinking Anthony would be outraged, I broke the news to him like a child telling his father he'd just hit a baseball through the windshield of the family car. Anthony calmly asked if I'd gotten the agreement in writing, which I had, and if I'd talked to the lawyer, which I also had.

He asked me a few more details before shrugging and saying, "Okay, so what's next on the agenda today."

Shocked, I asked, "Aren't you upset? That's twenty thousand dollars down the drain."

"No, I'm not upset. You did everything right. What's more, even if you hadn't, it's water under the bridge, so there is no point in wasting energy stewing about it."

I really got that lesson. Since then I've made plenty of business mistakes. First, I stop and learn from them. Then I keep moving. You can't let mistakes weigh you down.

The Ability to Execute Trumps Creativity

When I was young, I thought ideas and creativity were everything. But an incident when I was twenty-five years old helped steer me to the right path. I was working on a project to create a fun, interesting almanac. When I was a kid, I had loved reading almanacs, with their lists of populations and numbers. But all the almanacs were similar, and they were pretty boring. I had an idea to make a fun almanac. I worked on the project for about six months and called it "The People's Almanac." Sound familiar? A few months after beginning my almanac, I read in the *New York Times* about a famous author and his son who were working on an almanac. Like me, the son used to read almanacs and also found them dry. The duo was going to call their almanac "The People's Almanac." I was smart enough to know they hadn't stolen my idea. They just came up with exactly the same concept. I learned that there are millions of smart people in the world who notice the same needs and come up with the same ideas to fill them. Original, creative ideas aren't that valuable. What is valuable is your ability to execute them. The famous author and his son had the contacts and reputation to execute my—and their—creative idea.

Business Is Discipline

Anthony Harnett schooled me in the nuts and bolts of making a business work. He taught me the structural grounding, the discipline of business. And I mean discipline. When Anthony was on a store tour, he acted like a Marine Corps drill sergeant. He was famous for putting his fingers underneath counters and in the cracks of refrigeration units in search of dirt or bugs. No detail was too small for him.

Encourage Candor

Anthony and I fought all the time. We argued about everything from how to market the store to what employee benefits to offer. Anthony was imposing and intimidating, and I was one of the few people at the company who stood up to him. He didn't invite confrontation, but he knew that arguing his point helped him solidify his stance, so when we disagreed, we'd scream at each other at the top of our lungs. After a big blowup, we'd never stay mad for long. He appreciated my candor, and I respected him for keeping me around as long as he did.

The CEO Wannabe

In hindsight, I picked fights with Anthony because I wanted to run the business. I was struggling to make my mark, but Anthony was just as strong-willed as I was, plus he had a huge advantage: he owned all the stock in the company and I owned bubkes. I can see what I really needed was to start my own business instead of badgering Anthony about his. But as they say, hindsight is twenty-twenty. Later, when I became CEO of my own company, I realized what a tough job he had. Yet he made it look easy.

WHY I RARELY HIRE M.B.A.S

When I interview job candidates, it's not unusual for them to mention their M.B.A. One M.B.A. remark is okay, but if they shoehorn it into the conversation more than once, it's a turnoff. When I interview people enamored by their degrees, I doubt if they've got the chutzpah for the start-up world. The process of starting a business is sloppy, rough, and messy, and whether someone has an M.B.A. is the last thing on my mind. An M.B.A. is all about learning the structured and bureaucratic rules of business. Traditional business schools teach students to value position and lines of authority. Ironically, authority and bureaucracy are meaningless in the start-up world, where creativity, struggle, and sacrifice reign supreme. An M.B.A. won't keep you from succeeding as an entrepreneur, of course. The key is to understand the difference between the skills you studied in school and those you'll need to start a business. Not surprisingly, many of the world's greatest entrepreneurs don't have college degrees, much less M.B.A.s.

CHAPTER 5

Bike-Touring Adventures

*By the end of my cross-country journey,
I'd decided to become an entrepreneur.*

I felt like a fool as I watched the train pull away from the station. I was standing on the side of the railroad tracks at dawn in Kamloops, British Columbia, freezing. I kept a brave face as I waved good-bye to the friends I'd made during the two-day trip. But my smile faded as the last car disappeared. I took a deep breath and gazed at my surroundings. I was alone in a strange place with nothing but a few duffle bags and a cardboard box. The facts could no longer be ignored: it was the first day of my much anticipated cross-country bicycle trip, and I was woefully unprepared.

I hadn't counted on going solo. For years, a friend and I had boasted about taking the trip together. After separating from Bread & Circus, I was between jobs, a perfect time to make the dream a reality. Unfortunately, as my enthusiasm for the bike trip roared to life, my friend's sense of adventure fizzled. Unwilling to let him ruin my trip, I decided to go it alone. I bought a road bike, feather-weight camping gear, and detailed maps of North America's back roads.

Now, standing on a train platform two thousand miles from home, the first notes of regret began to sound in my psyche. I cast a doubtful look at the cardboard box at my feet. It contained the puzzle pieces of my touring bike. I had no idea how to put it together. The fact that I hadn't ridden a bike in at least fifteen years gnawed at my self-confidence. Since high school gym class, the most athletic thing I'd done was take out the trash.

I puttered around my belongings for an hour or so, opening the cardboard box and laying out the pieces of my bike on the train platform like a coroner conducting an autopsy. Staring at the collection of components, I couldn't even begin to imagine how to fashion them into a bicycle. I was about to slink toward the ticket counter to buy a return ticket when two brakemen carrying toolboxes strolled by. They glanced down at the discombobulated bike, then up at me. Whether they felt sorry for me or just wanted me off the train platform, I'll never know, but they offered to help me out. Thirty minutes later, bike assembled and camping gear neatly stowed in compact saddlebags, I wobbled down the street, listening to their good luck wishes fade behind me. Ten weeks and three thousand miles later, I steered into my brother Richard's driveway in Colorado Springs. I not only had learned how to survive on the back roads of America but also had met many of the hard-working, creative, small-town shop owners, salespeople, and entrepreneurs at the heart of American business.

Who Needs Madison Avenue?

Bike touring forces you to slow down and engage with your surroundings in a way that's impossible in a car. You notice an unbelievable amount of detail: the peeling paint on a roadside store, the astounding variety of mailboxes, and the subtle differences between early sprouts of soybeans, corn, and barley.

Each time I cruised through a small town, I stopped and introduced myself to local businessmen, especially owners of general or natural foods stores. This slowed my progress markedly, but I wasn't interested in speed: I was out to understand what made these stubborn small-town entrepreneurs tick. I was thinking about starting my own business and wanted to put myself in their shoes. No doubt they thought I was a little odd, riding up on a bicycle and quizzing them about their sales volume and customer service, but they welcomed my enthusiasm and were more than willing to sit down and share their business stories.

As I made my way across the country I learned countless business lessons, all of which would later come in handy when I started my own business in a small town in New England. In Skagway, Alaska, I saw one of the best marketing lines I've ever seen, on the side of a garbage truck: "Satisfaction guaranteed, or double your garbage back." What fun! And I bet they didn't lay out millions to a slick Madison Avenue firm for that slogan.

The Power of Hunger

When food is your only fuel, you learn the importance of filling up early and often. Sometimes your last meal is the only thing getting you to your next destination. I was a vegetarian at the time and fueled my way cross-country on grilled cheese sandwiches. I calculated I got about eight miles per sandwich.

When you pedal five to ten hours a day, you develop a jackrabbit's metabolism. I didn't chew my food as much as inhale it. I developed a reputation for cleaning out all-you-can-eat salad bars and wasn't surprised when I began to see "one trip only" signs posted at salad bars frequented by bicycling tourists. Other times I'd point to a pie for dessert. As the waitress started to cut a slice, I'd say, "No, don't cut it. I want the whole thing."

While riding through Idaho, I saw a good-sized town on my map and made it my destination. I'd planned on stopping, eating dinner, and spending the night. I peddled 65 miles to get to the place where the town was supposed to be, but there wasn't even a crossroads. I'd stumbled on a fake town. I learned the hard way that map publishers made up town names and printed them on their maps to catch thieves. If a competitor copied the map, they could prove it in court by pointing to the fake town name. That's how they protected their intellectual property. So there I was, starving and tired, standing in the middle of nowhere. There was no place to eat and nothing to do, and the next town was 55 miles away, which would put my day's total at 120 miles—much longer than I'd ever gone in a single day. But I had no choice. I was out of food.

The human body can do amazing things when it's hungry. It was dark by the time I rode into the nearest town. Sure enough, this was a real town complete with restaurants and stores, but everything was closed. I rode my bike past a diner and saw a guy inside mopping the floor. I knocked on the door. He mouthed that the restaurant was closed and waved me away. I kept knocking. Finally, he opened the door just wide enough for me to tell him my sob story. I begged him to sell me some bread. To my surprise, his face lit up, and he said, "No way am I going to sell you some bread. I'm going to make you dinner!" I told him I was into grilled cheese, and he made me ten sandwiches. He had so much fun. He flipped away on the griddle, and I ate everything he put in front of me. He'd never seen anyone eat that much in his life. That was just one of many times that summer I proved to myself I could accomplish the impossible. The confidence I built during that trip would prove to be priceless as a start-up entrepreneur.

Be Persistent: The Winds Will Change

You'd think the hills would be the biggest physical challenge on a bike ride, but winds are the worst. Bicycles are not very aerodynamic, and riding against the wind is like swimming against a strong current. You can spend hours going nowhere. It's the same when you start a new business: you often feel as if you're swimming against the tide. Perseverance is the only thing that will save you. It saved me while riding across Wyoming. The wind was so strong I thought I'd never make it out of the state. Then one day, I caught a tailwind so strong that I felt as if the hand of God was pushing me uphill. What fun to have the wind pushing me in a direction I actually wanted to go! I was twenty miles into Colorado before it died down.

Although winds are the worst, hills aren't far behind. When you're riding a bicycle cross-country, mountain passes are a major life event. It often took me half a day to get up a single pass. Many times when I reached a mountain pass, I would get off my bike and walk up to ten miles of steep grade, basically up the side of the mountain. But once I got to the top, not only was the view breathtaking but I got to cash in on the greatest reward ever: miles of zooming downhill without having to pedal. What a thrill to be cruising down those hills at forty-five miles per hour on wafer-thin bicycle tires, dodging every pebble and rut because if I hit one, I'd wipe out.

At the top of Chief Joseph Pass in Montana, I met a motorcycle gang. Motorcyclists call bicyclists "pumpers" because they think it's nuts to work so hard to power a bike. But these guys gave me an iota of respect for making it to the top of the peak with nothing but brute force. When they asked me if I wanted to ride down the mountain with them, I jumped at the chance. So we launched ourselves from the top—ten of them on Harleys and me on my bike coasting down the mountainside. I rode in the middle of the gang, enjoying the brief camaraderie of fellow risk takers. Near the bottom, we flew pass a recreation vehicle cruising along at thirty-five miles per hour. I watched as the driver placidly observed the first of the motorcycles go by, then caught sight of me whizzing by on my bicycle. He did such a big double-take that I thought he might run off the road. At the bottom of the hill, the motorcyclists gunned their engines, gave me a wave, and roared off, leaving me to resume my solo journey.

Never Stop Paying Attention

One day I was zooming down a Colorado mountain pass at forty-five miles per hour and soaking up the adrenaline rush that came with knowing that if I hit just one rock or one rut in the road, I'd be a goner. My mind was so focused on the pavement in front of me that it didn't register the fact that I was headed straight for a tunnel. As soon as the darkness enveloped me, I knew I'd made a potentially fatal error. This wasn't a fancy, well-lit tunnel on a major highway; it was a rickety structure thrown up to keep snow from burying the road. For the twenty seconds it took my eyes to adjust to its darkness, I was flying blind. There could have been a pothole the size of a Chevy, and I wouldn't have seen it until it was too late. I slowed down as much as I could without losing control, but it wasn't enough. I hit something—God only knows what—and the bike started bucking underneath me. Somehow I stayed on. When I finally slowed to a stop, I looked at the damage and saw the wheels were bent to nearly square.

Believe in Yourself

The daily risk versus reward of bicycling cross-country was the perfect training ground for my future as a start-up entrepreneur. During those ten weeks, I confronted challenges and jumped on opportunities. Every dangerous or unexpected situation put my problem-solving skills to the test. I had to rely on my ingenuity. Above all, the trip taught me to believe in myself. My bike trips gave me both the self-awareness and the confidence to strike out on my own in business. My willingness to abandon my comfortable lifestyle temporarily and put my safety at risk was a good sign I was crazy enough to be a serial entrepreneur. In the end, the hundreds of small successes I had on the road gave me faith I could survive on my own. It's not surprising that I started my first business shortly after my last bike trip.

CHAPTER 6

Building a Video Empire

*My perfect start-up: a hole-in-the-wall
video store.*

The year I responded to a classified ad in the *New York Times* advertising a video store for sale in Vermont, I was a desperate man. My career to date was nothing but a compilation of starts and stops: three years managing a rock band and six years off and on working at Bread & Circus and doing real estate. It was 1984, and I was living in Boston and calling myself a consultant. Truthfully, I was an unemployed and directionless thirty-six year old. Without a job, I struggled to keep some semblance of a routine. On weekdays, I rose, showered, and commuted to a friend's office, where I sat behind an empty desk and read the paper. I had a couple of job offers, but none felt as if they would satisfy my yearning for adventure.

I'd left Bread & Circus six months earlier. My battles with Anthony Harnett had become more intense, and it was clear he saw me as more of a competitor than a collaborator. I moved to New York and spent a few months on Wall Street working as an independent trader. The money I traded was my own. I made some profits, but I was still bored. My problem was I couldn't decide what I wanted to be when I grew up. I was bursting with creativity and eagerness, but as I'd learned at Bread & Circus, working for someone else wasn't my forte. I needed to strike out on my own.

My desperation to make something of myself not only drove me to finally start a business but also helped me to choose the perfect one. My fear of failure, along with my limited bankroll, forced me to make a logical and relatively conservative choice. Buying a hole-in-the-wall video store was not the most creative idea I've ever had, but in retrospect, it might be the wisest business decision I ever made.

How to Choose a Business

Jumping into the video rental business was a logical choice for several reasons.

It Was Profitable

It was the mid-1980s, video stores were a newfangled retail concept, and the industry was expanding at an unprecedented pace. Videos and VCRs were finally affordable. The latter had crept below the magic price tag of three hundred dollars, and people were snapping them up. Video store owners were raking in the money. Making a profit was easy in such a booming industry.

There Was a Low Barrier to Entry

I had $100,000 of bar mitzvah and inheritance money at my disposal. At its start, the video business was a rare opportunity for someone with relatively little capital (like me) to get in on the ground floor of something potentially huge. I haven't seen any concepts in the past twenty years be nearly as profitable as video retailing in the mid-1980s. The industry consisted of several small players, meaning we were all exploring this new concept together and were all on equal footing—at least for a while.

I Had the Right Experience and Interests

I knew a lot about both entertainment and retail from my experience managing a rock-and-roll band and working for Bread & Circus. I'd also been a movie buff all my life. I especially loved old classics and art house movies. This interest would differentiate me from my competitors.

I Had the Right Personality

Video retailing was the type of new industry that appreciated my creative approach to business. As industries mature, they grow stagnant and become less flexible. Creative minds become a less valued resource. But the video rental business was in its infancy, and when I bought my first store, I felt like an artist with a blank canvas. I hated the typical video store. Most of them were in ugly little shacks pushing rentals of X-rated movies and Rambo flicks. But I knew enough not to be put off by the competition. I knew I could vastly improve the video store status quo.

After taking stock of the business risks and opportunities, it seemed that the video store industry was the perfect place to start my entrepreneurial career. All I had to do was get in the game, so I gathered my courage, picked up the phone, and bought my first business.

Retail Is All About Location

Location is a deal breaker in the retail world. I'm not just referring to the east side versus the west side of town, although that's important, as we'll see later. I'm talking big picture. Before you start debating Park Avenue versus Lexington Avenue or Main Street versus Broadway, take a step back. Think about where your business will succeed on a national, perhaps even global, scale. Based on your strengths and weaknesses as well as those of your competitors, what's the big geographical context for your business?

When it came to my perfect start-up in the video business, I consciously chose to leave Boston for Vermont. I was afraid that if I opened a video store in Boston, I'd eventually be quashed by a Goliath-sized chain. This was early, so there wasn't a Blockbuster on every corner, but I figured it was only a matter of time. I also craved the connectedness that comes with a small community. I knew a video store could mean something to a small town in Vermont and serve the community in a way an impersonal, big-city store never could. Besides, Vermonters are notorious for cherishing and protecting their small businesses while rallying against chain stores like Wal-Mart. That kind of anticorporate venom is pretty appealing to a start-up guy like myself.

I settled on the small but booming three-season resort community of Manchester Center, Vermont. The local business district was a magnet for the smaller surrounding towns, and I had bought the only video store in the area. The store had one full-time employee, five hundred square feet, eight hundred tapes, and no parking. In other words, there was room for improvement.

Choosing the Right Part of Town

Now that I had carefully chosen the part of the country for my new business and had landed in Manchester Center, the next big location question was where in town to move my business. The store's biggest problems were location, size, and parking—meaning just about everything. It was on a side street, off the beaten path, and from the outside, it was just the kind of hole-in-the-wall video shack I swore I'd never own. But the size was a more pressing shortcoming than aesthetics. If another video store came to town with a bigger selection and better parking, I'd be sunk. Location takes on added importance in the video business because renting a video requires two trips: one to pick it up and one to drop it off. My big challenge was to find a location that was larger and closer to the town's main thoroughfare.

I set my sights on an empty gas station for my store's new location. The property was on the busiest road in Manchester Center, across from a popular shopping center. The spot was very visible and, even better, had plenty of parking. But McDonald's already owned the gas station and the neighboring property and was negotiating with the town to open a large restaurant on the combined properties. When I approached them about leasing the space, they turned me down. Reluctantly I kept shopping for other locations, but I couldn't shake the feeling that I'd already found the perfect place. Then one day I got a surprise phone call.

Vermont works hard to thwart big chain stores, and McDonald's had already waged a ten-year battle with the town to open its franchise. Having cleared many hurdles, McDonald's found one it couldn't overcome: Vermont's Act 250, which requires that business sites larger than one acre pass inspection by the state's stringent environmental commission. Desperate to avoid a further delay, McDonald's needed to sell the gas station to reduce the size of its property and called me. But if I was interested, I had to respond within twenty-four hours. Although I had to act fast, my experience with real estate told me that it was a great deal, and I snapped it up.

Nine months later, I opened my new store. It was a success from the start. Getting the best location in town was key. The new location was six times bigger than the old one and held nearly three times as many videos. We had twenty-five parking spaces and a bustling McDonald's next door. Business boomed. Soon I had the dominant video store in the county, and people visiting from New York, Boston, and Philadelphia regularly commented that it was by far the best video store they'd ever seen.

Make Your Customers Fall in Love

Location was not the only element of my success. It's one thing to get customers into the store; the trick is to keep them coming back.

A good video store plays an important role in a small community. On Friday and Saturday nights, everyone in town seemed to be in my store. They mingled, gossiped, and generally had a good time. After working at a grocery store, I enjoyed the playful atmosphere. Renting a video was fun; grocery shopping was a chore. For once, all of my customers smiled, and no one complained about the price of tomatoes.

When I had the store running smoothly, I began to expand our services and test some new ideas. Within a few months, I had racks of movies installed in general stores in the surrounding communities. Remember what I said about the importance of location for video stores? With smaller outlets, people could rent movies from the main store in town and return them to smaller stores closer to their homes. Making rentals and returns convenient for customers was good business sense.

Although we were in a small Vermont town, many of Manchester Center's residents were big-city refugees—a cosmopolitan bunch who demanded a variety of movies, like classics and foreign films, to keep their interest. We kept them happy by constantly rotating the movies among the main store and our ten general store outlets in nearby towns. Until our selection grew to be the best in the state, we also had a request system that included the entire inventory of another video store in Rutland, Vermont. The residents of even Vermont's smallest villages had access to a world-class movie collection.

Small towns offer up lots of public relations opportunities. Few people are more beloved in rural America than teachers, so I offered free movie rentals to all the teachers in the county for use in their classrooms. Teachers could call my store and request a video for a class, and we'd give it to them for free. This policy generated an enormous amount of goodwill. There wasn't a teacher within fifty miles of our store who didn't sing its praises.

Vermont's bad weather also presented a public relations coup. It only made sense that we waived late fees during big snowstorms. I'd go on the local radio station and tell our customers, "The roads are too dangerous to take your movies back. Stay warm and safe at home, and enjoy another night of movies on us."

I've yet to find a business that is more fun than a video store.

Don't Spend Money Before You Have It

With things going so well in Manchester Center, it wasn't long before I craved a bigger challenge. I felt great about my first store, but it still felt cramped. I decided sophisticated movie buffs needed a store big enough to carry ten thousand titles, and I envisioned a superstore with high-quality movies from all over the world.

I wanted to distance myself from the competition by catering to a more sophisticated level of moviegoers. By this point, Blockbuster was pioneering the movie superstore concept, but I wanted nothing to do with its cookie-cutter approach. Blockbuster was positioning itself as middle America's video store, which meant renting mediocre Hollywood movies to families and teenagers. I wanted to serve everyone else.

With that in mind, I went looking for a loan. I found a banker who was enthusiastic about the business and made several trips to the Manchester Center store. He assured me securing a loan for my superstore concept would be no problem. Taking his word, I signed a lease for a new location an hour away in Keene, New Hampshire.

I was several weeks into construction when he called with the bad news: I'd been turned down for the loan. Keene already had six video stores, and the bank president didn't think the town could support another. He apologized profusely, but nothing could change the fact that I was stuck building a video store I couldn't afford. I'd signed a lease and had a big obligation.

Mother Nature saved me from financial disaster. That summer it rained twelve out of thirteen weekends in Manchester Center. When it rains in a summer resort area, video stores do a huge amount of business. There were times when the shelves were empty because all of the movies had been rented. At one point, I even ran home and grabbed armloads of movies from my own collection to rent to our customers. Thanks to the rain, the original store did so well I was able to keep the new construction going for several months until I could secure bank financing.

The strategic lesson I learned that summer was that even well-meaning people make promises they can't keep. Since then, I've tried to live by the adage, "It ain't over 'til it's over." No one, not even bankers, likes to deliver bad news. Of course, it's in their best interest to be optimistic because they want your business. But it's a good idea to be skeptical when it comes to money, especially potential loans and investments.

Taking My Perfect Start-Up on the Road

Within a year of opening, the Keene superstore became the highest-volume video store in New England, and I recouped my $500,000 investment. Based on the success of my movie buff's paradise, I decided to roll out the concept. In six months, I drove fifty thousand miles looking for store locations in New England and upstate New York. I wanted towns with populations of approximately forty thousand—large enough to support a superstore but small enough to ensure my business would be the area's major entertainment center. The ideal location had to be convenient to the entire town, have high visibility, and provide parking for at least forty cars. In real estate jargon, I was cherry-picking—searching for that rare gem of a great location that would guarantee a high-volume store.

Because the territory was too big to cover single-handedly, I needed to grab the attention of the region's real estate brokers, so I sent them free videocassette recorders. Each machine was delivered with a note from me requesting just one thing: that the brokers call me first if a killer store location came on the market in their town. The VCRs cost roughly a hundred dollars each, while the locations themselves were worth hundreds of thousands of dollars. Of course, there were many towns that met my criteria where I couldn't get a toehold in the real estate market, but I needed to find only a few hidden gems. In the end, I sent out 120 free VCRs and as a result landed two great store locations—a fantastic return on my investment.

With a few smart tactics and a lot of determination, I got four more stores up and running in my third year of business. Each store had a minimum of five thousand square feet and an average of ten thousand tapes. My stores easily dominated the market share of every town we moved into: Poughkeepsie, Glens Falls, and Plattsburgh, New York; Leominster, Massachusetts; and Burlington, Vermont. On average, my stores had 70 percent of the video market in any one city, which was massive. By 1989, each store's revenues topped $1 million—more than five times the industry average—and the trade magazine *Video Store* listed Empire Video as the highest per store volume video chain in the country. I believe we were also the most profitable.

Revolutionize the Customer Experience

Most of my success came from the fact that Empire Video stores were unlike any other video stores people had ever seen. My Keene, New Hampshire, location, for example, was a sophisticated store designed for movie buffs. The interiors had high ceilings, warm track lighting, and sturdy wooden shelves with rounded edges that looked more like church pews than movie displays. The lettering on category signs looked handcrafted to instill a sense of intimacy. The categories themselves were unlike any you'd see at other video stores. Whereas our competitors had a handful of movie categories, we had more than sixty, including "Hardboiled Heroines," "On the Lam," "Swashbuckling," "So Bad It's Good," and "Science Gone Wrong." The store also had a mini-theater where up to eight people could sit in director's chairs and watch previews or clips of featured films.

I encouraged families to rent from my store not only by having the largest selection of children's movies in the state but also installing both a kids' play area and a pint-sized movie theater with small seats so children could watch the latest Disney movie while their parents browsed.

Customers loved the small perks our stores offered, like free phones. These were the days before cell phones, so picking a movie was a lot harder. If you came in for a movie and it wasn't on the shelf, you couldn't just call your spouse or kids and get their second choice. To make things easier, we installed phones in our stores for customers, and we encouraged them not only to call home but also, if we didn't have their movie, we gave them the phone numbers of our competitors to find out if someone else did. The numbers for the local pizza places were also posted so customers could order dinner from the video store. In a business like video rentals, all those little things add up to customer loyalty.

I love to surprise people. We passed out free locally grown apples in the fall, Hershey's Kisses on Valentine's Day, and roses on Mother's Day, plus free popcorn year-round for kids. The benefit of giving customers an unexpected gift, even a small one like free popcorn, was instilled in me when I was a kid handing out free popcorn at Miracle Mart. I did make one change, though: instead of giving kids popcorn on their way into the store, I gave it to them on their way out, which significantly cut down on my carpet-cleaning bills.

Ideally, renting a movie should be a coordinated effort between a knowledgeable staff member and a customer. To foster this relationship, I created a job description called "movie expert." This person's job was to circulate during busy times, recommend movies, and generally help people choose a film they'd love. I also put the workstation (the place where clerks checked in and organized movies for reshelving) in the middle of the store instead of in the conventional spot by the front door. I wanted my employees closer to the customers so they could recommend movies and answer questions. I outfitted the workstations with ten different movie review books so customers and employees alike could refer to the books when looking for a movie.

If staff members were going to recommend movies, the next logical step was to put my money where my mouth was. Whenever a staff member gave a customer movie advice, whether it was a personal recommendation or a staff review taped to the outside of the box, we guaranteed the customer would like the movie. Those who didn't like it got their next rental free. I knew the policy would endear us to our customers rather than cost us money. Plus, the constructive criticism helped us steer future customers away from bad movies.

One day a large, tall woman walked into our new store in Burlington, Vermont, looked me in the eye, and said, "I've been waiting for this store to open for months. I love foreign films, and no one else in town carries them. Where's your foreign film section?"

Deciding to tease her a little, I replied, "I'm sorry, but we don't have a foreign film section."

Her eyes narrowed, her fists clenched, and I thought for a second she might slug me, but instead she stomped toward the exit.

Before she reached the door, I added, "But we do have a French section, a German section, a Spanish section, an Italian section, a Russian section, a Chinese section, a Portuguese section, a Japanese section, and a Swedish section."

She whipped back around and broke into the biggest smile I'd ever seen.

When I ushered her to our huge array of French movies, tears of happiness streamed down her face. She bent down, picked me up off the floor, and gave me a hug. Making that woman happy was one of the most satisfying moments of my career.

Movie Matchmaking: The Heart of Our Business

My love of bringing people and movies together led to perhaps my greatest innovation thus far: movie matchmaking.

As I grew into my role as a video store owner, I wanted to design a store where people could easily find movies they would love. Pairing people with movies would be great for business because they'd keep coming back for more rentals. Keeping customers happy is important in any business, but in the video business, it's even more important because we were such an optional part of their lives.

There are a lot of other things people can do besides rent a video: watch television, have sex, or go out to dinner are only a few of them. You have to earn people's business by making the experience as positive as possible. Unlike bookstores where people come in to browse, read, and relax, video stores aren't places people want to linger. For the most part, they want to get in and get out as quickly as possible so that they can get home to watch their movie. Therefore, merchandising movies becomes an art.

How do you educate people quickly so they can easily find movies they will enjoy? My first step was to put my customers' desire for the truth about a movie above the studio's spin. To do that, we repackaged video boxes. We wrote our own reviews and taped them to the outside of the box, put sheets of paper inside a movie recommending other movies they'd like if they liked this one, and got creative with our categorization.

One of the things I liked most about the video business was the challenge of getting people to rent older movies. New releases are very expensive, so the profits are in older movies, classics, foreign films, and cult favorites. All media businesses—music, books, videos—are like that. New releases bring traffic to the store, but the business often loses money on them. Stores require many copies of a new release, and new movies were expensive—up to sixty dollars for each copy. Our high-volume store might initially need a hundred copies of a hit film, but once it had been on the shelves for a few weeks, the store needs only three or four of those copies. Since the value of new movies depreciates rapidly, the unneeded copies were sold at a big loss.

I loved recommending older movies to people. I enjoyed helping them discover films they otherwise would've missed. When I bought the store in Manchester Center, I purchased hundreds of older releases. To match customers with movies they'd enjoy, I also purchased three thousand copies of Leonard Maltin's thousand-page movie review book. For the next several months, I gave one away to every customer who walked in the door. The books, which cost us four dollars each, generated thousands of rentals because people were able to identify older titles they'd like. I found a way to do what I love: helping people while making money too.

Movie matchmaking guided our marketing and in-store promotions too. We were always running film festivals for different genres and promoting "sleepers" and "movies you might have missed." Ours were some of the first video stores to have an employee-recommendation section. Our staff loved promoting their favorite picks.

Attract the Right Employees—and Train Them Well

The headline of our help-wanted ads was always "A Movie Lover's Dream Job," and it was true. My video stores attracted the best movie talent because I treated my employees like royalty. I knew that if I treated them like kings and queens, that's how they would treat the customers. Once the company became profitable, I paid them extremely well—more than any comparable job. On top of that, I offered unprecedented benefits, including profit-sharing bonuses twice a year.

The smaller perks also added up. On busy days, managers brought food and refreshments in for the staff. Positions were rotated to prevent burnout. And employees were given free dinners for doing their jobs well. We handed out roughly five to ten free dinners in each store every week, and many times the manager gave the entire staff free dinners. And, of course, employees had access to free movies.

I was and remain a fanatic about ensuring good customer service in my stores. My staff went through extensive training when we opened a new store. We had a mandatory series of four training seminars on topics such as dealing with new customers, handling on-the-job stress, defusing customer complaints, and recommending movies. I made the classes fun with role-playing exercises and plenty of free pizza. Every employee also received two detailed training manuals. The first was an introductory booklet that explained backward and forward that the customer is always right. The second was a more detailed twenty-page customer service guide given after an employee had completed a few weeks on the job. The booklet was filled with specific examples of what to do when faced with various scenarios, such as when a customer says he returned a movie but the store's computer can't find it. The employee was trained to say, "No problem, our mistake," and to note the discrepancy on the customer's file. We had a three-strikes-and-you're-out policy. If the same customer reported three times that he or she had returned a video that our system reported as still missing, this person got the boot.

Make Customer Value Profitable

To succeed in a big way, figure out how to offer your customer the most value while still pulling in as much profit as possible. I achieved this balance at Empire Video. In particular, our movie-buff superstore business model was both wildly profitable and customer friendly. Thanks to our movie-matchmaking culture and enormous selection, we rented a large percentage of older movies, which are very profitable. Conversely, we rented fewer new releases, which are loss leaders. At the time, the average video store spent 35 percent of its revenue on new releases. Empire spent only 20 percent; consequently, our net profit margin was double that of our competitors.

Matching customers with older movies wasn't just profitable; it added significant value to the customer experience. No other video store in town could match Empire Video's film selection, customer service, and movie information.

Our competitors weren't just not matching our offerings; they were inept. Except for Blockbuster, big players stayed out of the video business at first because they thought video on demand would make video stores obsolete before the year 2000. As a result, our competitors were small players who made a lot of money between 1984 and 1987, when video retailing was so easy anyone could succeed. As the industry got tougher, most of the hole-in-the-wall stores couldn't cut it. An easy-entry industry that grows as fast as video did creates a glut of marginal players who fall out later. In Keene, my competitors were so clueless they still charged new customers a club membership fee of fifty dollars. Empire Video did just the opposite: new customers got a free membership and two free rentals just for walking in the door. A year after Empire Video opened in Keene, four out of our six competitors were out of business.

My Perfect Start-Up, with Lessons Learned Along the Way

Don't Underestimate the Value of Good Technology

Technology is my Achilles' heel. I've never been computer savvy, and I've hobbled every one of my businesses by mismanaging technology. My first technology mistake was hiring someone in Vermont to create Empire Video's computer system. He was a local guy and very hands-on, but he didn't have the expertise the job demanded. My second mistake was not keeping an eye on him. I don't deal well with techies. The details of what they do drive me nuts. I knew we had computer glitches and that the company's record-keeping system was awful, but I didn't know what to do about it.

One of the most crippling effects of bad technology was an inability to collect late fees. When I discovered our computer system wasn't properly recording late fees, I thought, "No big deal. Our stores are in small towns, and people in small towns are honest, so it won't be an issue." Boy, was I wrong. It turns out that everyone hates late fees. As soon as our customers discovered our weak spot, they capitalized on it. I lost my shirt over late fees. The concept of renting property and bringing it back was still novel. People weren't used to being held accountable. Just the phrase "late fees" implies criminal behavior. People didn't like having us call them at home and tell them to bring our movies back. When we finally put in a new computer system and began accurately tracking late fees, our revenues went up 15 percent, and our profits doubled. Technology glitches stunted Empire Video's growth by at least a year.

One crazy video store owner I knew in Connecticut collected his late fees with a gun. If his customers refused to respond to phone calls, he'd grab his gun, go to their homes, and demand his movies back. Of course, that's an extreme case, but those VHS tapes were expensive; for rare movies, a video store retailer would pay upwards of a hundred bucks. If a customer lost a tape or the dog ate it, it got expensive.

Creativity and Compromise Don't Mix

On a less vital scale perhaps, I think the name Empire Video was also a mistake. The investors I brought in to help me expand the chain loved the name because it made sense on many levels. For one, we knew we'd be opening a lot of stores in upstate New York, so there was a nice empire connection. Plus, the Star Wars trilogy was a huge hit, so there was a fun duality in the word *empire*. We also thought *empire* fit our stores because they were so big. Granted, all three of us chose the name, but I was never happy with it. The name wasn't bad, but it wasn't an attention getter, which can give a new business an extra boost.

The name Empire Video lacked originality. I'd had another name I liked much better: Lost Planet Video. Of course, this was before the word *planet* became as commonplace as it is today. Twenty years ago, the word was creative and fun. It also worked well visually. I even came up with a logo of a planet with Saturn-like rings. But I ended up with a blasé name because I compromised rather than sticking to my conviction. A strong brand comes from one person's clear vision, not from a group consortium. But choosing a lackluster name was the least of the problems that hatched from my investment partners.

When Expanding, Choose Investors Wisely

Expanding from the two stores in Manchester Center and Keene to six stores throughout New England and upstate New York did not come cheap. I had managed to open my first two stores with my own money, but I needed investors to expand the chain. I'd accumulated all the debt I could handle. I chose an old friend from college and a friend of his to invest in the company. Mixing friendship and business was a huge mistake. Lots of people do it because it's tempting to seek help from people you trust. In addition, starting a business is so stressful, you need the emotional support. But I'm here to tell you: don't.

We immediately got off on the wrong foot. My friend and I were at odds over what his role was going to be in the business, and the third guy caused trouble from the start. Instead of bene-fiting the business, our conflicts stifled the company's growth. Eventually things got so ugly that we went through three arbi-trations trying to solve our differences. At the time, I blamed them for the whole mess. With the wisdom of hindsight, how-ever, I realize I was part of the problem. I was a poor communi-cator, and my methods were unconventional enough to make most people nervous. My bad relationship with my investors was one reason that by 1992, I decided to sell the business. But my contentious relationship with my investors wasn't the only rea-son for deciding to sell—or even the most important.

CUSTOMERS CAN BE YOUR BEST TEACHERS

If I had to boil down my thirty-plus years of business wisdom into a single lesson it would be this: get to know your customers. The seeds of my biggest business success—creating a $100 million dot-com—were sown by getting to know my customers at my first video store.

Back then, I dusted the shelves, swept the floor, and worked the cash register. While doing the grunt work that goes into run-ning a small business, I also got to know my customers. By watch-ing them, talking with them, and asking about their likes and dislikes, I gained insights I later built on to develop movie match-making, a concept that has since made me rich. But I never would have conceived of movie matchmaking if I hadn't been working on the front lines.

One day I was working the floor when one of my favorite cus-tomers came to me with a request: he wanted me to recommend a comedy he could watch with his friend who needed cheering up. "This guy desperately needs a good belly laugh," he said. "I want a sure thing." I was sure I had the perfect movie for him. I'd just seen Raising Arizona, a movie produced by the Coen brothers, and I thought the film was a riot. I assured the customer that he and his friend would laugh themselves silly. The next day, the guy stormed back into the store waving the cassette. "I can't believe you gave me this idiotic movie," he spat. "I was so embarrassed; I turned it off midway through!" I was astonished at my poor judgment. That moment sparked my obsession with the science of matching customers with movies. That's why so many movie executives are left scratching their heads when a sure-fire hit flops at the box office. Unless they've worked in a video store, they can't possibly understand what drives people to see certain movies. Quentin Tarantino attributes much of his success to his start in the business as a video store clerk.

CHAPTER 7

Millionaire Without a Mission

I struck a deal with Blockbuster, headed for Silicon Valley, and left small-town retail behind forever.

One day, when I still owned Empire Video, I struck up a conversation with a woman sitting next to me on an airplane. During the cross-country flight, small talk turned to career confessions. She'd climbed the corporate ladder but wasn't happy with her life. She'd lost sight of the spark that initially attracted her to her job. When I asked why she stayed in a position she didn't enjoy, she said it paid well and had great benefits. So I asked what she would do differently if she had a million dollars. How would she follow her heart? Our chat got me thinking about my own life. Then it hit me: I'd completely lost my enthusiasm for Empire Video. The tedium of running a regional chain of video stores had extinguished the spark that attracted me to the business six years prior. But unlike her, I wasn't stuck. Slouching back in my seat, I absorbed my reality. I had a million dollars in the bank and could do whatever I wanted. Financial pressure was no longer an excuse not to follow my dreams. For the rest of the flight, I digested this revelation.

Strange things happen when you accomplish your mission. Becoming a millionaire and therefore financially independent had been my focus ever since I watched my father lose his business and most of his wealth. Now that I'd met my goal, I felt a profound sense of relief as well as an instant loss of direction. I had a million dollars in the bank, but I felt empty. Luckily I was in a good spot for self-exploration. The video stores were mostly running themselves, so I had time and energy to explore who I was and what I wanted to do with my life.

Answers to those questions didn't come easy. I was successful, but I was alone and insecure both as a person and as a businessman. I had built a business, but it was a regional retail chain similar to what my father and uncles had done. I felt safe in the familiarity of small-town retailing. I didn't believe I could succeed in business on a national scale.

But at least I'd had enormous professional success, which is more than I can say for my love life. I was making a half-million dollars a year from Empire Video, but I couldn't sustain a healthy, loving relationship. After the fateful plane ride, I adopted the Beatles' song "Can't Buy Me Love" as my theme song. I was forty years old and my love life consisted of nothing but a string of short relationships. I craved companionship, but I hadn't come close to finding a woman with whom I could spend the rest of my life. My loneliness kicked off my quest for a psychotherapist.

Learning to Heal

Some people would rather live in misery than seek therapy. Not me. I've always seen therapy as an important tool of self-discovery. Perhaps I'm open to the idea because my older brother, Marv, is a psychotherapist. I'm open, but that doesn't mean I'm easy. My search for a therapist took years and involved a dozen of false starts and strange encounters. One guy started to twitch whenever our talks turned serious and kept redirecting the conversation to lighter fare. Another was obsessed with Sigmund Freud and couldn't stop blathering about him. Finally, in 1991, I met Sonia Nevis, a sixty-three-year-old psychotherapist and well known teacher of Gestalt therapy.

Sonia's kindness disarmed me. I immediately felt comfortable telling her the most intimate details of my love life and my childhood. She helped me see that I was reliving bad relationships from my lonely and insecure childhood through unhealthy romantic and even business partnerships. She showed me how to heal the pain from my childhood so I could move on with my life.

The results were unequivocal. First, I was finally able to sustain a long-term relationship with an incredible woman, Diana, who became my wife.

Second, I let go of Empire Video. Although I'd lost interest in running the chain, I felt a paternal obligation to its employees and customers. Until Sonia helped me let go, I kept asking, "What will happen to them if I sell?" I still had nightmares about deserting my friends in the James Montgomery Band.

Sonia helped me become a genuine serial entrepreneur. She suggested that perhaps I should make my living starting new businesses since I enjoyed it so much. She gently pointed out that before I could start new businesses, I had to learn to let go of the old ones.

A third outcome of my work with Sonia was gaining the self-confidence to try my entrepreneurial skills on the national and even international stage. In time I would throw myself into the twentieth century's California Gold Rush: the dot-com boom.

When I found Sonia, my love life was chaotic and my business life was ho-hum. Two years later when we finished our work together, the equation was reversed: my love life was happily secure and my career was more stimulating. Without Sonia, I never would have become a dot-com multimillionaire. But that story comes later. First, there's the matter of how I sold Empire Video to the only buyer that could afford the chain: Blockbuster.

Seducing a Giant

Thanks to Sonia, I was emotionally prepared to embark on a new mission in my work life. I decided to use movie matchmaking to catapult my ideas to the next level. But I had no desire to build a large national company myself, so I set my sights on partnering with Blockbuster, the only national video chain at that time. Yes, I wanted to cash out and sell Empire Video to them, but an even bigger motivator was my desire to connect millions of people with great movies. I hoped to revolutionize Blockbuster's mainstream culture from within by infusing it with my movie-matchmaking spirit. But first I had to get the attention of the company's executives. I hatched a plan that would both get their attention and start our relationship on the right foot. I didn't want to call them; I wanted them to call me.

Therefore, I sought out and landed a cover story about Empire Video in *Video Store,* the nation's biggest video trade magazine. I knew as soon as Blockbuster's executives read about Empire Video, they'd want to find out more. Why? Because my stores were much more profitable than theirs. They would want to know what made Empire Video tick. Sure enough, two days after the issue premiered, Blockbuster's senior vice president, Bob Garron, called and asked, "What are you doing tomorrow?"

Playing it cool, I answered, "Well, if you want to come up, I guess I could make some time to meet with you."

"No, I want the whole day," he insisted. "I want to see your stores."

"That's great, but we can't do all the stores in one day. It's too much driving."

"I'll tell you what," he said. "I'll pick you up on my private plane, and we'll see them all in the same day."

The Blockbuster jet was waiting when I got to the Keene airport the next morning.

My feelings were mixed as Bob and I hopscotched across New England checking out my stores. What was a 1960s radical like me doing on a corporate jet? The more I talked with Bob, the worse I felt. He told me he'd been an FBI agent before joining Blockbuster and that his father had been a special assistant to J. Edgar Hoover. But as the day wore on, Bob's Irish charm overcame my apprehension. He was great with the store managers who picked us up at each airport. He took a personal interest in their lives and genuinely valued their dedication and honesty. Many times over, he confided in me that he wished his company's managers were as talented and committed. By the end of the day, we'd formed enough of a friendship to give each other a little ribbing. I accused him of being more right wing than Attila the Hun, and he called me a bleeding heart liberal. In the end, we both laughed at each other and at ourselves.

That visit generated a series of buyout negotiations between myself and Blockbuster's number two in command, Scott Beck. After weeks of back-and-forth, I thought we had a deal, but at the last minute, Blockbuster executives got cold feet and killed it. Instead of a merger, as I'd hoped, Scott offered me a job as a consultant. That wasn't what I'd hoped for, but it was still an opportunity to take my ideas to a national audience. That's how I became a high-level consultant for Blockbuster. During that time, I helped merchandise existing stores by breaking categories into smaller movie groupings, as we'd done at Empire Video. I sat on their "store of the future" committee. And most important, I brainstormed how to usher movie matchmaking into the digital age.

I have Scott Beck to thank for dragging me into the computer age. He forced me to learn about computers. During several meetings that lasted well past midnight, he convinced me that the future of both movie matchmaking and customer education was in cyberspace. I will always be grateful to him for pushing me toward technology. For that reason, among others, he is one of my most important mentors.

Back in the early 1990s, the Internet was in its infancy, and neither Scott nor I knew exactly what the Web was. But we did know a technology revolution was coming and we needed to get on board. He brought in Intel and IBM as partners, and we got a prototype high-tech Blockbuster up and running. The new store had information kiosks where customers could look up movie information, read reviews, and watch previews. The kiosk interface was very similar to today's Web sites. We didn't know it at the time but we were designing what would become my next business: Reel.com.

Soon after we completed the experimental store, Scott left Blockbuster to buy Boston Chicken. Shortly after, Blockbuster shut down work on its information age stores. Consequently, my consulting job was over. Seven years later, they asked me to restart the project, but it was too late. I'd started my own dot-com.

Learning What Fits

After it became clear my Blockbuster consulting days were over, I looked for another project to sink my teeth into. I pursued everything from buying an alternative weekly newspaper to creating fruit-juice-based sodas. After an intense six-month search

I thought I'd found the ideal business: an educational-themed toy store.

I was passionate about the project. Educating and entertaining the kids of baby boomers felt like a great mission. But giving birth to a new business concept while running the video stores was next to impossible. My employees resented the new venture. They made it clear to me that they'd signed up for the movie business, not the toy business. Trying to get them to switch back and forth between the two was confusing and frustrating for everyone. In the end, I learned an important lesson: don't start a business entirely different from the one I'm already running. But the idea was a good one. The start-up's project manager asked my permission to take the idea to another company. I gave him my blessing. He retooled the idea into a toy company called Noodle Kadoodle and built a good-sized chain.

Taking My Music to Jamaica

Between 1989 and 1993, I was often bored and restless. I wasn't interested in being the CEO of a mature, midlife video store chain; my consulting with Blockbuster was short-lived; and my other business ventures stalled. The one creative outlet that didn't fail me during those years was my music, a hobby that was becoming more and more important to me.

Since my early days with the James Montgomery Band, I had dreamed of becoming a musician, but it wasn't until I met Matt Solon that I dared to think my dream might materialize. I met Matt at a party shortly after moving to Vermont. During our conversation, I told him I played the harmonica. He jumped up and said, "I've finally found my harmonica player!"

As it turned out, Matt was starting a band and needed a harmonica player. I insisted he wait to hear me play before offering me the gig, but he was undeterred. "You're the one," he said. "I can feel it." Matt's group was called the Vermont Secessionist Blues Band. He was the band's guitar player, singer, and songwriter. He took me under his wing and turned me into a real musician. For the next nine years, we played in bars all around the state. The local radio stations even made a hit of our trademark song, "Free Vermont."

I also fed my inner musician during those years with frequent trips to Jamaica, where music plays a large role in the culture. Hail a cab at the airport, and the driver may have to take the door off its hinges to let you inside, where you'll probably sit on bare springs, but as soon as the radio comes on, you'll be treated to a state-of-the-art sound system. Of course, people associate Jamaica with reggae, but most Jamaicans prefer country-western. What fun to be in the middle of Jamaica and hear nothing but country crooners. Because I always carried my harmonica with me and favored rural areas instead of tourist magnets, Jamaicans saw me as a musician, not just another "white mon." My harmonica became entrée into the local music scene. During a concert, all I had to do was wave my harmonica above my head and the musicians would yank me up on stage, give me a microphone, and off I'd go.

The Sale Is Made

Music was a wonderful outlet, but I needed a new professional venture to captivate me. And Empire Video needed a new owner. Bored and restless, I was starting to make dumb mistakes, like almost losing one of our stores because I forgot to renew the lease. I was no longer working with Blockbuster, but I'd stayed in touch with Bob Garron. One day, out of desperation, I just picked up the phone and said, "Bob, do you want to buy some stores?"

At that time, Blockbuster dominated the industry. The next ten video store chains combined didn't equal Blockbuster's heft. Blockbuster was the only one that could afford the Empire Video stores, and they obliged. The price wasn't high: $3 million. Nearly half went to me, the other half to my two investors. The sale dragged on because Blockbuster was in the midst of negotiating its sale to Viacom. But finally, on January 2, 1994, Blockbuster took Empire Video off my hands, and I was free to embark on a new adventure—one that took me far away from the snow-covered mountains of Vermont.

The Joy of Vermont

Although I left New England for good in 1994, the nine years I had spent in the Green Mountains set the stage for the rest of my life. Vermont was home, a beautiful safe haven for me to heal and find myself.

In a way, Vermont was ideal for me. The contrast of busy days and secluded nights suited my personality. I got a daily adrenaline rush by running the video stores. At night I retreated to the country for peace and quiet. I owned a home on twenty acres with the nearest neighbors a quarter mile away. My house sat on the edge of a small lake. I could jump right from my deck into the water. At night, the sky was filled with stars.

I also fell in love with Vermont's people and culture. Nothing sums up the state's quirkiness better than my experience with its highway patrolmen. I did a lot of speeding along the back roads. As a result, I had regular contact with the highway patrol. One time I got pulled over for a broken brake light. After the patrolman explained to me why I was getting a ticket, he motioned me to step out of the car. At this point, I was getting a little nervous. But he stuck out his hand and said, "Hi, my name's Lionel Shapiro. Nice to meet you." Then he told me what it was like to be the state's only Jewish highway patrolman. I guess he didn't often get a chance to talk to other Jews. We talked for half an hour about Vermont and how the governor wasn't giving the highway patrolmen any money and how Lionel had to work out of his house and missed the camaraderie of other patrolmen. At the end of our chat, he handed me my ticket. Later I wrote a song about him called "The Legend of Lionel Shapiro."

A New Adventure

Thanks to my psychotherapist, Sonia, I was able to let go of Empire Video. Leaving the fate of my employees in the hands of a big chain was painful, but I needed to move on. And for the first time in my life, I started to believe I could create something on a national scale.

Although I had more confidence and self-esteem than ever before, I needed a break from running a business. For nine years, I'd been responsible for the livelihoods of more than a hundred people. Starting a big business requires 100 percent energy and drive, and I wasn't quite ready to launch a national entrepreneurial effort.

But I was ready for adventure and, as always, I needed a lot of stimulation. As it turns out, the adventure I chose, joining the

professional high-stakes poker circuit, would also help to pre-
pare me for more success than I could imagine in the high-stakes
world of Silicon Valley.

DECISIONS SHOULD BE MADE BY THE PERSON WITH THE BEST RÉSUMÉ

What makes a successful start-up is vastly different from what
makes an established company successful. One leadership rule,
however, applies to all companies: let people with the best
résumés make the decisions. Of course, a company's leader ultimately must take responsibility for the decision, but the best leaders let themselves be heavily influenced by advisers with the
appropriate experience and training. This approach isn't always
easy, especially for someone with an entrepreneur's ego. Entrepreneurs often find it difficult to put decisions in other peoples' hands.
At Empire Video, I made all of the decisions because I was too
insecure to share my power. Now I know that my job isn't to know
everything but to identify who will know best. These days I dele-
gate decision making to the person with the best résumé. More
important, once I pinpoint the right person for the job, I abide by
his or her decisions regardless of whether I agree with them. Of
course, I first make sure the person has the expertise to back up
his or her opinion. And I'm not afraid to put the question out to
more than one person. In the end, if I get conflicting opinions from
two different advisers, I inspect their résumés even closer to deter-
mine whose advice I should heed.

CHAPTER 8

My Professional Poker Career

*After two years of high-stakes poker,
I was ready for anything.*

For the next two years, I made my living playing on the high-stakes poker circuit. The lessons I learned from competing against the best poker players in the world continue to influence my career on a daily basis. I consider the time I spent playing professional poker the equivalent of earning my M.B.A. The demanding dog-eat-dog atmosphere of the high-stakes poker scene prepared me not only for being a better entrepreneur but also for surviving the cutthroat world of big business. A lot of business books talk about poker as a training ground, but my perspective is much more personal.

The first poker player who took me under his wing was my grandfather, Simon, who had a legendary reputation as a card shark in Akron, Ohio, and beyond. I was a product of 1950s middle-class suburbia, but my family was hardly Ozzie and Harriet material. My grandfather stopped by our house on his way to poker games. When I heard his car pull into the drive, I'd race up to my room, raid my piggy bank, and come back with five dollars. He'd take the money with a nod and a promise to make good on my investment. After a day at the tables, he'd return with my share of his winnings. I could usually count on pocketing ten or fifteen dollars, big money for a ten year old in 1958.

I put my winnings back in my piggy bank. My grandfather, skeptical of banks, liked to bury his in the backyard. I remember coming home from school one day to find rows of soggy twenty-dollar bills drying on laundry lines in the backyard. Apparently the bags had sprung leaks, and my parents, uncle, and grandfather had frantically dug them up to keep the cash from turning into compost.

Playing poker vicariously through my grandfather instilled in me an early love of the game. Like a lot of other guys, I played amateur poker in my twenties and thirties. But it wasn't until I sold Empire Video that I played professionally. The choice was a natural one for me: I needed a break from business, but I craved stimulation. Poker gave me the adrenaline rush without the responsibility of running a business.

I went to San Francisco in 1994 and became a regular at the Bay 101 casino in San Jose. Although I wouldn't recommend this path to everyone, I'm convinced that I learned more about business in two years playing poker than I would have in any M.B.A. program. Before playing professional poker, I'd spent my time in the relatively genteel world of small-town business where people looked out for each other and deals were made with a nod and a handshake. Poker toughened me up and honed my business skills, making it possible for me to enter the national playing field. Here are the important lessons I took away from the tables.

Choose Your Game Carefully

When it came to both amateur and professional poker, I learned early on to be picky about what game I sat in on. Back in my early thirties, while riding my bicycle cross-country, I peddled into Eureka, Montana, a small town—population one thousand. As I steered my bike toward the campground, I spied a sign in the window of a local bar: "Poker Game Tonight." I hadn't played in awhile, and I missed the camaraderie, so I decided to put my poker skills to the test. I couldn't have known I would learn a crucial business lesson that night.

When I arrived, I noticed most of the players were locals, mostly mill workers and lumberjacks. But one guy stood apart from the crowd. He was immaculately dressed in a white suit. Diamonds flashed from his fingers, and gold graced his wrists. He introduced himself as a poker player from Texas. What he didn't say, but we all knew, was he'd come to take our money.

Here was a guy who'd chosen his game carefully. He'd driven fifteen hundred miles from Texas to Montana, and he wasn't in town for the wildlife viewing. He knew the odds of winning in Texas were long. Poker had been popular in the state for years, and the players were shrewd. In contrast, the game had been legal in Montana for only a few months, and no one had the foggiest idea how to play, including myself.

Round after round, the Texan stretched out his manicured fingers and swept our chips into his growing pile. He dominated the table with charm and skill. He was polite and helpful to a fault, especially to the biggest losers. I lost about a hundred dollars, big money for me at the time, but the experience was such a thrill I didn't care. Later I lay awake all night replaying every hand in my head and dreaming about becoming a professional player someday.

Now that I'm older and wiser, I know the Texan was simply a skilled businessman out to earn a buck. I'm still not sure if he was a good poker player or a great one. But it didn't matter. Relative to our game, he was fantastic. That's what I call context, and it's the key to making good business decisions. To win at poker, you've got to know a lot more than when to hold 'em and when to fold 'em—you've got to decide whether you belong in the game.

I relied on context when choosing where to locate my first video store. I was living in Boston at the time and knew I wouldn't be able to compete with the inevitable arrival of national chains in the city. So I moved to Vermont where people hate chain stores and I had enough capital to build the biggest and best video store a small town had ever seen.

Don't Play with Money You Can't Afford to Lose

During my time on the high-stakes poker circuit, I rarely played in games beyond my means. That discipline gave me an advantage over many players who were better than me, especially the young bucks with big egos and small bankrolls. Of course, every rule is meant to be broken.

The one time I got in over my head was one of the most thrilling experiences of my life. The game was at the Bellagio, the fanciest gambling venue in Las Vegas at the time. Each bet had to be either one or two thousand dollars. I approached the table because it looked like easy pickings. A rich guy was throwing his money around and playing every hand. But it wasn't as easy as it seemed. Before I knew it, I'd dropped thirty thousand dollars. Angry at myself for being out of my league, I decided to ride it out a few more hands. That's when my luck changed. My opponents were dealt six bad hands in a row, and I got twenty thousand dollars ahead. With my heart thumping out of my chest, I gathered my chips and walked away. Sure, I made some money, but the experience was so scary I never did it again. The notion of losing everything wasn't what frightened me; it was the addictiveness of the adrenaline rush. I was afraid I'd get hooked and never look back.

In that way, poker is a great money management lesson. You have to manage your money carefully because cash flow problems jeopardize every part of your game. If the guy sitting next to you thinks you're losing, he won't take you seriously, which makes bluffing nearly impossible. To make matters worse, when you're losing at poker, your confidence evaporates. If you lose your self-assurance, you'll undervalue your hand, and the odds of failure go sky high. The same goes for business: if you don't start off with enough capital, the business will flounder and you'll find yourself making decisions for the wrong reasons.

Money does funny things to businesspeople. Some won't shutter a failing business or toss out a bad strategy because they've invested too much money and are afraid to change direction. But money already lost shouldn't keep you from altering your plans. Just like knowing when to fold 'em in poker, you've got to know when to get out of the game and salvage what you've got left. Don't think about the money you've lost; think about the money you haven't spent yet. Great poker players always abide by this rule. No matter how much money they have in the pot, they'll throw their cards away if the odds turn against them.

One of my worst business mistakes was putting money I couldn't afford to lose into my latest business venture, Elephant Pharmacy. The minute the first store opened in Berkeley, California, I knew my adventure was going to be very expensive. I spent nearly every penny I had to keep the business running. Unlike a good poker player, I miscalculated the financial risk of entering the game.

Hope for Good Luck, Plan for Bad Luck

Watch a few poker games and you'll see how luck plays out. On a bad-luck day, great players can lose a lot of money. And with a little good luck, even horrible players can rake in the chips. Ultimately the balance between good luck and bad luck drives the game because a little short-term luck gives mediocre players the ego boost they need to stay in the game, which means the great players will eventually mop the floor with them.

The best poker players have the patience to wait for good cards. As a result, they play only a fraction of the cards they are dealt. Players who insist on playing every hand can occasionally win big but more often than not lose big. For three months, I watched a lousy poker player called Harpo terrorize the high-stakes games in northern California. He looked like a tall Harpo Marx and was almost as funny. Over the years, playing every hand cost him a lot of money, but when he was on a winning streak—watch out!

I'm a big believer in budgeting bad luck into a business plan. When you're starting a new business, undoubtedly something will go wrong. I sometimes think that Murphy's law was invented for the start-up world. So much is out of your control, just like a poker hand. One way to fend off bad luck is to choose a lucrative business, as I did when I was starting Empire Video. In 1985, video stores were booming, and a lot of entrepreneurs were getting rich; even those with little to no business savvy were making it big. It was a perfect situation for me because I was a trained retailer and was competing against people who had no idea what they were doing.

Some people say you make your own luck through hard work, and to some extent that's true. The more you try to do something, the more likely you are to succeed. Like a spider, the bigger your web is, the more you'll catch. Still, you shouldn't count on hard work alone. Sometimes, no matter how much you toil away, you're going to have bad luck. Likewise, good luck brings success to some people who don't earn it. After all, people win the lottery every day.

Know the Difference Between Luck and Talent

Some famous businessmen like Bill Gates, Warren Buffett and Steve Jobs have so much talent they don't need luck. But unless you're one of these types, you'll need both luck and talent to be successful. I've enjoyed my share of good luck, but I also have a natural talent for business. Still, sometimes it's hard to know where one ends and the other begins.

In poker, as in the rest of life, your ego can get dangerously big when you confuse luck with talent. I once had an incredible winning streak during a month-long poker game in Dawson City in the Yukon. I returned to Boston thinking I was really hot. With thoughts of my winning streak filling my sails, I jumped into casino-level games. In no time, the cash I'd won the month before was gone. I hadn't become a great poker player in the Yukon; I had just gotten lucky and let my ego get the best of me. Distinguishing between luck and talent is important in the business world too. But discerning the difference between the two can be tricky.

During the dot-com boom, a lot of entrepreneurs, including myself, made a lot of money we didn't deserve. In the early years of the digital mania, I founded a company called Reel.com, one of the first online video stores, and sold it two and a half years later for $100 million. When strangers asked me how it felt, I told them it was like winning the lottery. Although Reel.com was a great company, I knew I didn't deserve to earn that kind of money. I was simply in the right place at the right time.

I kept telling myself it was luck and I shouldn't get overconfident, but I didn't heed my own advice and grew arrogant. My egotism led me to pour half my profits and $10 million of other people's money into my next start-up: Hungry Minds.com. The result was a disaster: the company failed, the investors lost their money, and my ego took a well-deserved beating.

Identify Your Strengths and Weaknesses

My weaknesses as a poker player were almost insurmountable. That is one of the reasons I'm so proud of becoming a winning, high-stakes player. For starters, I have a horrible memory, I am not observant, and I lack discipline. My sloppiness often led me to misread my cards or flash them to other players while I was distracted. Worst of all, I'm not aggressive or predatory by nature. I like to nurture people, not eat them for lunch. None of this boded well for my poker career.

Ironically, understanding my weaknesses saved me. I knew I would never be the best poker player in the world, so I wasn't coming from the big ego place that hobbles many talented players. Instead, I approached the table with humility and self-awareness. When I saw I was the worst player at the table, I'd think, "Wow, this is going to be very expensive; I better go do something else." And I'd get up and leave. My lack of a poker ego allowed me to be objective about my strengths and weaknesses, which gave me the foresight to play at appropriate games with appropriate people.

It may sound counterintuitive, but one of my biggest strengths is that I'm not a gambler. Professional poker players approach the game as a business. They recognize that gambling is bad for business. That's not to say professional poker players don't gamble. When they feel the urge, they'll shoot a game of craps or bet on their favorite sports team. They gamble away from the poker table. They understand that gamblers are destined to lose because to gamble is to rely on luck instead of facts. The professionals cash in by waiting for gamblers to come along.

Be Ready to Leap

Poker also taught me the value of opportunism. Maybe your winning hand tanks and the opportunity is to get out before you lose more money. Or your losing hand suddenly becomes a winning hand and you need to capitalize on the turn of events. The intense pace of a poker game is similar to that of the start-up world. To make solid, split-second decisions, you need to be in touch with both your instincts and the logic of the situation. The challenge is to stay balanced between being too cautious and too aggressive. You can't let your excitement cloud your judgment.

When I opened Empire Video in Manchester Center, I had a lousy location, but real estate was scarce, so I took what I could get. Still, I coveted a building that stood next to what would become a McDonald's. I tried to rent the space for months to no avail. Then one day, out of nowhere, the owners called and offered to sell it to me. The catch was that I had to buy it that day, and I jumped on it. Had I not learned the value of opportunism at the poker table, I wouldn't have had the confidence to recognize the break and grab the property.

Play the Players, Not the Game

Great poker players don't play the cards; they play the other players. The key to being a successful poker player is knowing how to read people. This is especially pertinent when you're playing the pros. At a certain level, the card game is irrelevant. Everyone at the high-stakes tables is an equally good card player. Most regular players master the pot odds and mathematical expertise within a couple of years. But what separates the winners from the losers is knowing your opponents and knowing what they know about you.

There are three ways to play the players in business.

Treat Every Exchange as a Negotiation

Every poker hand is a give-and-take with an opponent. Are they bluffing? Are they telling the truth? Similarly, in the business world, you've got to know your adversaries. What makes them angry? Are they afraid? What makes them overconfident?

Once I was negotiating with a man from Texas about the sale of a video store, and he could sense a weakness in me: that I desperately needed to sell the store to pave the way for a much larger business deal. And no matter what I did, this guy kept calling and changing the terms of the contract to his advantage. He was playing hardball, and I was letting him get away with it. I finally decided I'd had enough—it was time to bluff. The next time he called, I told him I didn't appreciate his attitude and to "f*** off." Then I hung up on him. He called right back and said we had a deal. I'm not saying you should be rude or use foul language, but there does come a time when you may need to call an opponent's bluff with a bluff of your own.

Study the Competition

Amateur poker players learn the ins and outs of the game by observing other players and studying their moves. In the business world, you have to borrow moves from people who know more than you; otherwise, you're forced to reinvent the wheel, which is very expensive.

Before I started Elephant Pharmacy, I spent a lot of time studying Walgreens. For the life of me, I couldn't figure out why they devoted so much floor space to greeting cards. Cards alone are not a moneymaker and take up a huge amount of space. What a waste! When I visited Walgreens during the Christmas season, the cards suddenly made much more sense. People buy cards because it's a holiday or a birthday, which means they are often in the market for a gift too. So I put a large greeting card section in Elephant Pharmacy. Sure enough, the cards helped sell candles, yoga mats, and CDs, all with high profit margins.

What if there are no businesses to study? Say you've done your homework, canvassed the landscape, and no one is doing what you're proposing. Usually that's bad news, which means you should take a step back. There are millions of smart people in the world. We all have access to the same information and therefore all hatch similar ideas. Most likely, there are reasons that someone has not already capitalized on your idea. Figure out what the roadblocks are before you get started. When I was in the planning stages of Elephant Pharmacy, everyone told me it was the best business idea they'd ever heard. That made me highly nervous. If it was such a good idea, why wasn't someone else doing it?

Believe What You See, Not What They Say

Poker is a game of deception, so lying is the norm. It's a game of knowing what someone else has in his hand, knowing what they think you have, and acting on that information. In business, if I'm feeling that someone isn't telling me the truth, I look at the situation with a poker player's skepticism. Don't get me wrong—I'm not a skeptical person; I like to give people the benefit of the doubt. But in the business world, sometimes that can be a handicap. I'm proud of my ability to think like a poker player. For example, I often put on my "poker hat" during job interviews. Getting to know an applicant quickly is almost impossible. The situation requires making an important decision based on gut feelings.

Time to Move On

After two years of playing full-time professional poker, I learned my lessons. Poker is a brutal business. People will take your money in a heartbeat if you let them. Poker is not a business with heart and soul. Sure, some poker players have wonderful personalities and are charming, but they are not creating something that adds value in other people's lives. Giving something meaningful and valuable to people satisfies me on a very deep level, and those two criteria form the foundation of my business philosophy.

Another reason I stopped playing poker is that it no longer satisfied my yen for new challenges. The games themselves were challenging, but I no longer wondered if I could make a living as a full-time poker player. I was a success, which meant the challenge was over and it was time for me to move on. I don't play poker anymore but I use the lessons I learned at the poker tables every day.

THREE RULES TO WINNING IN POKER AND BUSINESS

All successful poker players and entrepreneurs use a combination of the same three strategies to win.

Be Aggressive

Aggressive poker players win by scaring other players into making mistakes. In business, one way to succeed is to scare your competitors. Wayne Huizenga, the only person to create three Fortune 1000 companies, embraces aggressive business tactics. When he started his first company, Waste Management, he steamrolled into towns and offered to buy out the owner of the local garbage collection business. If the person refused to sell, watch out! Wayne was famous for being a ferocious competitor. Thanks to him, Waste Management went on to become the largest garbage company in the world.

Play Tight

In poker, "tight" means you bide your time. The goal is to wait until you have great cards before playing, so your odds of winning are much better than those of people who play every hand they are dealt. In business, this practice translates as being conservative. For instance, opening up a franchise might be a smarter move than starting a company from scratch. Aggression and conservatism are not mutually exclusive; you've got to find a balance between the two and know when to use each.

Hone Opportunism

Poker demands an ability to jump on an opportunity at a moment's notice. Likewise, in start-ups, being opportunistic is essential. Half of succeeding in business is being in the right place at the right time; the other half is recognizing that time when it comes. My experiences playing poker sharpened my sense of when to leap at an opportunity. Had poker not taught me the value of opportunism, I never would have had the courage to buy an important piece of real estate for my Vermont video store on one day's notice.

CHAPTER 9

Easy Dot Come

The Making of an Internet Pioneer

How I founded and sold a company for $100 million in less than three years.

I learned a lot during the two years I spent playing professional poker, but I was itching to do something new. I wanted to jump back into the start-up world, and I knew exactly what company I wanted to start. During my nine years in Vermont, I'd become obsessed with what I call movie matchmaking, the art and science of delivering valuable movie information to customers. Thanks to Scott Beck at Blockbuster, I knew my future would be digital, so it felt like a natural transition for me to migrate from the world of brick-and-mortar businesses to cyberspace.

In the mid-1990s, there was only one place to be if you wanted a future online: Silicon Valley. Ever since spending the Summer of Love on Haight Street twenty-five years earlier, I had known I wanted to end up in northern California. So in 1994 I packed up and moved to San Francisco. While sharpening my negotiating skills at the poker table, I absorbed all the information I could about the Internet. I carried the first issue of *Wired* magazine around with me for a year, reading it so many times that it fell apart. It was my new bible. Most of my friends thought I had gone off the deep end because I wouldn't stop talking about my digital fantasies.

I leveraged my experience with Empire Video and Blockbuster to start one of the first online video stores, Reel.com. My dream was to create the world's biggest source of videos and movie information. With a worldwide market, we could have hundreds of thousands of movies. I envisioned a future free of headaches about real estate, parking, and square footage. And I was convinced that movie matchmaking would make Reel.com the coolest site on the Web.

Start with What and Who You Know

In 1996 I started Reel.com in an unassuming office building on San Francisco's bustling Market Street corridor. My staff consisted of family members and long-time friends. One became a consultant; his wife became my secretary. A friend's daughter, a recent Stanford graduate, became my assistant, and my older brother acted as my Internet guru. Although he's a psychotherapist, not a businessman, he was a crucial adviser during those early months. He sat with me for hours in front of his computer screen patiently showing me how to use the Internet and giving me tours of the hottest Web sites.

Reel.com was heavy on theory and short on pragmatism. We lounged on the floor discussing existential questions: What is Reel.com? Is it a store? Is it an information service? Should the company be an information-only site, a retail site, or a combination of the two? This navel gazing went on for months, and I enjoyed every minute of it. In many ways, rumination is my greatest strength; it allows me to focus all of my creative energy into the start-up.

Six months later, we concluded that Reel.com needed to be in the movie sales and rental businesses. But my heart was still in education, so we decided that the sheer breadth of our movie information would set us apart from other video stores. Once we had a business model, it was time to rally investors.

A Dot-Com Is Born

I phoned all my business friends, including Anthony Harnett, from Bread & Circus, and Scott Beck, from Blockbuster. I easily gathered $2 million—half of it mine—to start Reel.com.

The initial funding allowed me to hire graphics and technology people to bring the Web site to life. With more staff, Reel.com was resembling a substantial business; it also meant we needed more space. I went looking for real estate near San Francisco's South Park, the epicenter of the city's Internet heyday. I fittingly found a fifteen-hundred-square-foot space two blocks from the offices of *Wired* magazine.

In the early days, every Internet company was a concept company—a company that appears big from the outside but doesn't consist of much on the inside. Running a concept company is like being the Wizard of Oz: you look larger than life, but if someone pulls back the curtain, he or she will expose you for what you are—a scrawny guy yanking on wires, pushing buttons, and yelling orders into the phone. My favorite example was Amazon.com. Jeff Bezos started the now-world-famous Amazon .com with little more than a wing and a prayer. His business plan was simple: buy a sales list from the world's largest book wholesaler, put it online, and advertise as the world's biggest bookstore. In the beginning, he was just a guy sitting in an office trying to convince the press, the public, and some venture capitalists that Amazon.com was going to be huge. He was probably selling a few dozen books a day at first, but the concept was brilliant.

Reel.com started as a hybrid: half dot-com, half brick-and-mortar. My thinking was that a Web site would be unprofitable for many years because the Web was so new and expensive. From my experience at Empire Video, I knew a large brick-and-mortar video store catering to sophisticated movie buffs could be a cash cow. The physical store would generate profits as well as build Reel.com's online brand.

We opened our giant video store, also called Reel.com, in Berkeley in June 1997. The store had many features, including the largest selection of videos in the country divided on the shelves into four hundred subcategories and high-tech kiosks for movie information. I wanted to open more physical stores, but the Internet took off so quickly that our venture capitalists wanted Reel.com to put all of its resources online. Everyone sang the same chorus: "The Internet's taking off like a skyrocket. You have to get on board with both feet." So I did. But it was a shame. When Hollywood Video bought us later, they said that we had the most profitable brick-and-mortar video store in the country. Ironically, the location of our Berkeley store had been a Hollywood Video that had never been allowed to open by the community.

My VCs Wanted Their Money Back

Within four months of our initial round of financing, Reel.com had burned through most of the $2 million I'd raised. Half the money went to building the physical store; the rest disappeared into the Web site. I knew I needed more cash to keep the company on track. I needed venture capitalists. So I approached CMGI, a Boston-based Internet company that owned both Lycos and GeoCities. Peter Mills and Dave Wetherall, CMGI's partners, had an almost childlike enthusiasm for both movies and Reel.com. They loved talking about their favorite films and what movies they thought would be popular among online buyers, and they eagerly invested roughly $3 million in Reel.com.

CMGI's investment triggered a growth spurt for Reel.com. I moved the offices to a funky former car dealership close to the Berkeley store and stocked up on inventory so we could say

Reel.com had the largest movie selection on the planet. We created a business development department to make partnerships with other companies, and we invested in our technology. I poured money into the company's infrastructure, but like shoring up the foundation of a house, it didn't look as if we were making much progress from the outside. As our bank account shrank, CMGI's representatives got nervous.

We burned through the $3 million in venture capital money so fast that CMGI suspected we'd swindled them. Fearing the worst, they sent auditors to our offices. At one point, CMGI threatened to call their lawyers. My explanation was simple: we'd invested the cash in Reel.com's future, and they would see it pay off soon.

Thanks to our investment in a public relations media blitz, they didn't have to wait long: our business tripled in less than a month. Within weeks, CMGI went from threatening me to congratulating me. When they expressed interest in buying my share of Reel.com for $20 million in CMGI stock, I wasn't interested. A year later the stock offer I'd rejected was worth nearly $1 billion.

Investors Can Come from Unlikely Places

With a money-hungry dot-com start-up, the search for more funds and new investors never ended. For example, my staff told me stories about a wacky guy named Paul who called the customer service line to debate facts about obscure movies. They were amused and impressed by his detailed knowledge. Only later did we find out that our mystery caller's last name was Allen. Thanks in part to our great customer support, Paul Allen, cofounder of Microsoft, fell in love with Reel.com and became the company's fifth-largest stockholder.

Our other big new investor came as a result of illness. I was scheduled to give a speech in New York City at a conference for Internet companies. It was my chance to represent Reel.com and myself to the richest venture capitalists in the world. The timing couldn't have been better: Reel.com was on shaky ground, and we needed investors badly. But I had a terrible case of the flu, and someone even had to help me onstage. Halfway through my speech, I was so tired that I stopped talking and gazed out at the audience. I couldn't believe what I saw: people on the edge of their seats. Afterward I got my first standing ovation. I couldn't figure out why I'd been such a hit. As it turned out, I was so sick that my words had come out much slower than usual. People actually heard and understood what I was saying. Usually I talk as fast as I think, and people can't keep up. I haven't given such a great speech since.

The next day I went to visit Herb Allen, possibly the most successful backer of large companies in the country. I met with his second-in-command, Jack Snyder. As soon as we shook hands, Jack asked me, "How much money do you want?"

"Well, gee, don't you want to get to know us better?" I asked.

"I had two people at your speech yesterday," he told me. "I know everything I need to know. How much do you want?"

So that's how I got the backing I needed, and Reel.com survived to see another day.

Know Your Limits

Reel.com was three businesses in one. The first was a mail-order video business. At first, we sold a lot more movies than we could handle. We didn't have the staff to figure out what we were doing wrong, much less the necessary computers and equipment to handle the mushrooming number of orders. The second business was movie information. To that end, we had writers and freelance movie experts who developed original content and movie matchmaking for the Web site. We used the quality of our information to attract movie lovers to the site; then we sold them videos. The third business was the physical store in Berkeley. The physical store and the online store had a symbiotic relationship. The store had computer kiosks directly linked to Reel.com's Web site. Therefore, customers could access movie information from the Web site while looking for a video to rent in the physical store.

As Reel.com grew, so did my responsibilities. I juggled all three businesses single-handedly and struggled to keep up. I felt as if I had three CEO jobs, and that was just the beginning. Reel.com was so threadbare I did all the marketing, hiring, and fundraising myself. I even wrote some of the more difficult movie reviews.

I'm a better start-up entrepreneur than a manager, so once I had the three businesses up and running, I approached my investors and told them we needed a new CEO. My candor took them by surprise. Most entrepreneurs are famous for refusing to hand over the reins once they have exhausted their usefulness, but I'm forthright about my strengths and weaknesses. I knew the company needed someone else for the long haul.

We hired Julie Wainwright to replace me as CEO of Reel.com. I moved into the chairman's seat and tapered my involvement with day-to-day operations. Wainwright was exactly what Reel.com needed. She had honed her marketing and management skills at big companies like the Clorox Company. She also had experience managing start-ups. Her leadership infused Reel.com with the credibility in the business community to go to the next level.

Big-Time Marketing on a Small-Time Budget

The secret to success at Reel.com was public relations. At first, I was stymied. Opening up a business on the Internet was like starting a business on the moon. How did I tell people who we were and where to find us? How could I drive customers to my site? Some Internet companies got the word out by broadcasting commercials during the Super Bowl. Others plastered their Web site addresses on the Goodyear Blimp. But we didn't have that kind of money. Our total budget for two years of advertising, public relations, and marketing was a half-million dollars. We had to get creative.

After intense cajoling on my part, I convinced the country's hottest Internet-focused public relations agency to accept us as a client. The firm, Neihaus Ryan Wong, was known for building the Apple and Yahoo! brands. Over the next eighteen months, their twenty thousand dollar monthly fee ate up 80 percent of our marketing budget. It was worth every penny. Thanks to their media contacts and credibility with the press, articles about Reel.com began popping up in magazines like *Wired* and *Business 2.0*.

The media buzz helped to allay CMGI's fears. More important, it did wonders for our cash flow.

I would do anything to get publicity for Reel.com. When my mother needed minor surgery and no other family member could help, I went to Los Angeles to be with her. I decided to do a little business while I was in town and set up some interviews. The day of her surgery, I was waylaid at a radio station waiting to be interviewed. The producer delayed my spot again and again, but I stuck around. I was so focused on getting publicity for the company that I missed my mother's surgery. (She still hasn't forgiven me.)

A *Titanic* Promotion

Wainwright's biggest coup was our *Titanic* promotion. In the weeks before the video release of the blockbuster hit *Titanic,* we hit the airwaves with advertisements hawking the video for the unheard-of price of $9.99. Every newspaper story about the video's impending release included a mention of Reel.com as having the best deal around. As a result, Reel.com got more than 270,000 online orders for the movie. Of those customers, 70 percent had never bought a video online before. The campaign was a huge success. The only catch? The video's wholesale price was seventeen dollars. Reel.com lost seven dollars with every sale. The escapade cost the company more than $2 million. But Reel.com was mentioned in virtually every newspaper in the country. You can't buy that kind of press. Plus we had scored tens of thousands of "virgin" video-buying customers who could be mined for years to come.

Good Writing Gets Results

Reel.com's good, clear, fun writing attracted customers. Customers want information fast, especially online, and they want to make efficient choices. We had to convey a lot of information in very few words, a skill I'd honed at Empire Video. Whether they are online or in a brick-and-mortar store, shoppers have a short attention span. Our writing was short, honest, and user friendly, such as, "Art house critics loved this movie, but mainstream critics thought it was too slow." We wrote and rewrote every review to make it both brief and insightful.

Be Prepared to Put Your Money Where Your Mouth Is

You never know what's going to strike a nerve. One of our early ideas the press latched onto was "Cinema U." In press releases, we described it as a virtual film school where customers could attend lectures, watch films, and have class discussions online in one of three dozen college-level courses. Our tagline was, "Where nobody graduates." Cinema U was only a pipe dream when we sent out the press release, but the media loved the concept so much we had no choice but to develop it—fast. In the end, we offered a handful of courses, including screenwriting, Americana Cinema of the 1970s, and the Hong Kong New Wave. We charged students $24.95 each, plus film rentals. Although it was never a moneymaker, Cinema U more than paid for itself in media attention. Although we did many things right at Reel.com, we also made some serious mistakes.

My Most Expensive Mistake Ever

My lack of technological savvy has cost me dearly in each of my business ventures. But at Reel.com, the cost of my incompetence may have cost me $1 billion. Getting a Web site as complex as Reel.com up and running (much less keeping it that way) required nothing short of rocket science. Software designers couldn't keep up with how quickly the Internet was evolving, and finding good Web techies, even in Silicon Valley, was impossible. Adding to the challenge was the fact that I didn't understand technology management in the first place.

The fact that Reel.com was a Web favorite made our technology problems even more heartbreaking. People loved our Web site, but it crashed all the time. Some days it crashed more than a hundred times. Our techies ran around trying to manage one crisis before the next but never fixed the glitches long term.

Every day when I walked into the office, bad news greeted me: "The Web site crashed twenty times last night," or, "The site hasn't worked for two hours," or, "A writer from *Wired* magazine called, angry because he was trying to write a review of our site and he couldn't get on it." The feeling was akin to being smashed over the head with a baseball bat.

Early in the dot-com craze, Jeff Bezos and I toyed with the idea of merging our companies. I confessed to him that I was screwing up the technology end of Reel.com. I told him, "I'm not a techie." He puffed up his chest and said, "Me, I'm a techie." That difference in our personalities is mirrored by the fates of our companies.

When it was up and running, Reel.com was one of the coolest and most original sites on the Web. Here was movie matchmaking on an unprecedented scale. With our patented "Anatomy of a Movie," we dissected and rated every film according to fourteen elements ranging from sex and violence to action and soundtrack. Each element was graphically represented on the site so customers could quickly judge if a movie was high on action, middle-of-the-road on language, or low on romance. We also rated all the critics' ratings and had proprietary movie information systems that made the pickiest movie buff happy.

Customers could choose from more than eighty-five thousand films in seven thousand categories ranging from "Science Gone Wrong" to "Cerebral." The database was searchable by title, director, and actors. For $4.50 plus shipping, customers could rent a VHS tape and have it delivered to their door. (This was long before Netflix made this service standard.) But if you peeked under the facade, you would have seen the truth: the site was held together with little more than shoestring and gum.

Reel.com's technology problems were not limited to Web site crashes. We also had big problems with other systems, including our ordering system. I still have nightmares about our worst disaster: the system crashed and was down for two days during our first holiday season. At least six hundred orders vanished. We had no way of alerting the customers. People may still be wondering what happened to their order.

The Deal That Got Away

My other weakness is speed. Refusing to slow down cost me one of the biggest business deals of my life. Reel.com had a very important relationship with the London-based company IMDb (Internet Movie Database). The company had a huge amount of information about movies and a great business model where their customers supplied a lot of the information. Any detail you could imagine was on this site, such as who the second makeup director was on a movie fifty years ago. We integrated substantial parts of our site with theirs and cosponsored events like film festivals.

I wanted to buy IMDb, but I couldn't afford it. Instead I planned to solidify the partnership by visiting their offices and offering to trade some stock. But I postponed the trip over and over again because three days of travel felt as if it would slow me down too much. Then one day I got news that Jeff Bezos at Amazon.com had flown to London, met with IMDb's executives, and bought the company. I couldn't believe it.

Reel.com continued to be a success, but I can only imagine how much bigger it could have been. I found out later that Jeff feared Reel.com would be too powerful if we partnered with IMDb, so he pulled the rug out from under us. He later told Julie Wainwright that we were one of his toughest competitors.

We Didn't Know We Were Getting Rich

In the early Internet days, the scene reminded me more of Haight Street than Wall Street. There were more idealists in Silicon Valley than get-rich-quick types. We all knew that the Web would dominate business someday, but none of us expected it to happen so soon. We were just a bunch of struggling start-ups trying to look bigger than we were.

David Rasher, the number two executive at Amazon.com, was visiting Reel.com during a week when his company's market capitalization jumped from $500 million to $700 million. "That is just a short covering rally," he said. "There is no way our company is worth that much." But Amazon.com's stock kept going higher almost every week for many months. It didn't stop until it reached a market cap of $40 billion in 2001. Likewise, my venture capitalists, CMGI, saw their long-dormant market cap go from $500 million to $70 billion in less than two years. Nobody had any idea that was going to happen.

A Hollywood Ending

During Reel.com's first two years, I ran through two-thirds of my life's savings. Not surprisingly, I came close to pulling the plug many times. Between the Web site and the physical store, I often felt as if I was going broke with no chance of turning things around. Although mine had a more conservative business plan than most other dot-coms, I still thought I had bitten off more than I could chew.

You could say that divine intervention saved Reel.com, just like rainy weekends saved Empire Video. But this time my savior wasn't Mother Nature; it was the stock market. The business world turned inside out, and investors threw money at dot-coms. The more money a company was losing, the better, or so it seemed. And Reel.com became very popular.

Several members of our board wanted to make an initial public offering for the company. I hated the idea for two reasons. First, I felt we would end up cheating our new investors since Reel.com was not yet well positioned to survive on its own. Second, I was sure a big crash was inevitable and wanted to cash out beforehand. I took a strong position to stop the IPO. I told the board that if they insisted on the IPO, I would personally tell the public not to buy the stock—strong words coming from the company's chairman and founder. They got the message, and we cashed out.

I knew Reel.com needed to be part of a larger company when we were told to stop opening our profitable brick-and-mortar stores. The Web site was just too expensive to operate without the cash flow from those stores. The two companies I identified as good merger candidates were Blockbuster and Hollywood Video. I thought both would want an online presence and be looking to partner with an established dot-com like Reel.

With the help of Scott Beck, who was close to executives at both Blockbuster and Hollywood Video, we received buyout offers from both companies. Blockbuster offered to partner with us and divide the online proceeds fifty-fifty. Hollywood Video offered $100 million in cash. I leaned toward the Blockbuster deal. But Julie, our CEO, and others in the company preferred the Hollywood Video deal. Having been so close to going broke six months earlier, I was grateful for any deal at all.

Reel.com was still a facade, not a profitable business. Our burn rate had grown to sixty thousand dollars per day with no end in sight. That's how weird it was doing business during the height of the Internet bubble. We made the deal in June 1998 and closed that September. I owned only 17 percent of the company's equity (investors and employees owned the rest), but I still pocketed $17 million—not bad for less than three years of work.

A Time to Celebrate

Being rich gave me the freedom to do some spectacular things. After selling Reel.com to Hollywood Video for $100 million, I took a six-month hiatus. My job during that time was to throw myself one amazing fiftieth-birthday party.

I celebrate milestones in larger-than-life ways. A decade earlier, for my fortieth birthday, I'd organized a virtual college reunion in Vermont with all of my friends. Now with my fiftieth birthday approaching, I was eager to celebrate with my friends and family, many of whom had also made a bundle with the sale of Reel.com.

With my heartfelt connection to Jamaica, it seemed only fitting to host a Jamaican celebration. And my birthday is in November, the best time of year to visit Jamaica because it's before the holiday rush and after hurricane season. So I arranged to rent the majority of rooms at a beautiful little beachfront hotel. Diana and I flew down two months prior to the event to relax and put our plans in place.

I invited sixty people, and fifty came—a fitting number for the occasion. The group included everyone from Scott Beck, the executive from Blockbuster, who arrived with his wife and six-month-old baby, to my eighty-two-year-old father. Dad was nearing the end of his life and suffering from Alzheimer's disease, but he still appreciated a good time. He was the life of the party. He loved music and had played the violin and percussion instruments in his younger years. Although his illness had made him less mobile, that week he danced the entire time.

The emphasis of the week-long party was music. Musicians from both California and Jamaica played day and night. Guests could jump in and play the conga drums or bongos even if they'd never played a musical instrument in their lives. Day after day the sun warmed us, the water cooled us, and we danced, played reggae music, and ate the best jerk chicken in the world. The music infused the party with a Jamaican spirit, and by the end of their stay, more than a few party guests had dreadlocks and beaded braids. As my wife and I escorted groups of guests to the airport, we sang them a special parting song we'd written: "The Last Day Blues."

DO'S AND DON'TS FOR CHOOSING A BUSINESS

During my career, I've started four intentional businesses and a couple of unintentional ones. Through it all, I've learned a lot about what it takes to pick a winner. Here is some food for thought:

Base your decision on logic, not emotion. Many people let feelings and passion steer them toward a business, but don't let your heart call the shots. Starting a business is a logical decision. Stay focused on the important questions: Who are you? Where do you fit? Who are your competitors?

Stick with the familiar. Choose something that feels comfortable. If it doesn't feel like a natural fit for your skills and personality, pick something else.

Prioritize fun. If you don't enjoy your work, you won't succeed. Look for a business with the potential to be deeply satisfying. You are about to dedicate your life to this business, so it better be something you love. If your customers see you having fun, they'll keep coming back.

Choose a business within your grasp. The desire to create your ultimate dream business right away is tempting, but you need to start small. Think of your first business as a stepping-stone to bigger and better things.

Enter an established field. If your business idea is 100 percent original, there is a reason that no one else is doing it. Look around at what other businesspeople are doing. What works for them, and what doesn't? Both mistakes and innovations are best learned by watching others make them first.

Know your risk tolerance. Make sure you pick a level of risk that is appropriate for you. Various businesses have different levels of risk. For instance, a franchise can be very low risk because everything has been worked out. Creating a new business model,

however, is extremely risky. How much risk can you accept and still sleep well at night?

Focus on short-term goals. Don't get ahead of yourself. Forget about designing a business for the next decade; instead, design it for the next year. If you're already envisioning your business as a successful national chain, take a big step back. How will you get there? How does the business ramp? How will you get through all the early hurdles to establish yourself? The small bumps in the beginning are usually more treacherous than the large obstacles down the road.

CHAPTER 10

Easy Dot Go

Getting Carried Away with the Internet

Good intentions but a lousy business plan is a great way to lose millions.

After returning from Jamaica, I knew I wanted to do something spectacular in the business world. I wasn't motivated by money (I had all the money I could ever want). I was motivated by the desire to use that money to build a business that would help people's lives. After my unexpected bonanza at Reel.com, I felt an obligation to give back. I believe in the saying, "For those to whom much is given, much is required." I had won the lottery and wanted to share my good fortune. I decided to start another dot-com. The trick was finding a dot-com idea that would somehow resolve the problems of people who needed help. But what problems and which people?

Find a Mission for Your Venture

In early November 1998. I called Sandy Sickley, with whom I had worked at Empire and Reel.com, to help me develop a new concept. We spent almost two months kicking around various ideas with different people before settling on online learning.

From the beginning of history, education has been the key to freedom and power. If you're born into a very poor family, your best chance of making a great life for yourself is through education. For first-generation Americans, the American dream includes a chance for their children to become the first in their families to go to college.

My goal was to help spread access to education through modern technology. We wanted to create the Web's dominant online learning portal and store for distance education. We planned to sell online courses made by others and eventually create our own digital classes.

Hungry Minds.com, the wonderful name Sandy developed for our new venture, would be the premier site for online learning. The Web site would carry classes offered by universities, like the University of California at Berkeley extension, and other organizations, like *Money* magazine, on every topic under the sun. Best of all, people could learn at their own pace. I wanted customers to pick and choose what type of class best suited their personalities: fast or slow, visual or audio, reading based or animated.

Don't Forget the Bottom Line

Education tailored to an individual's attributes and personality was an important concept to me. I had had a hard time in school because I didn't fit the rigid mold of the successful student in the 1950s and 1960s. I wanted to help others avoid the frustrations I had faced.

What I learned from Hungry Minds.com is that good intentions in business don't contribute to success. No matter why you are starting your business, you better have a plan that will make a profit. In the English language, the expression *bottom line* refers to the fundamental, unavoidable core requirement or demand of any situation. That general expression comes from business, and I learned that the hard way at Hungry Minds.com: the bottom line in business is the bottom line.

As we developed Hungry Minds.com, I was too focused on helping other people and didn't pay enough attention to making a profit. That's not a good idea. Unless you are focused on profit when you design your business, it will probably fail.

I started Hungry Minds.com to give something back to society. I even planned to donate all of my stock from the new company to charity. That's a nice sentiment for a businessperson—but that businessperson better make sure the stock is worth something first.

Haste Makes a Lot of Waste

Benjamin Franklin was dead on: if you rush something, you're just going to make a mess.

There were two reasons that I never bothered to create a viable business plan for Hungry Minds.com—a plan that would delineate specifically how we could turn our concept into profit. The first reason, as I said, was that I was too focused on the "good" that I was doing to worry about whether I was doing "good business." The second reason I launched Hungry Minds.com without a workable business plan was haste. I was in a hell of a hurry. The reason for my haste wasn't impatience; it was my conviction that the dot-com boom, which had made so many people very rich (including myself), was about to implode.

Every forty years or so, the financial markets go insane as the prices of stocks from favored industries skyrocket. An equally big crash always follows. I lived through the speculative bubble in the late 1960s when the stock market had a boom and a bust similar to the big one of 1929.

In 1999, the dot-com bust was clearly on the horizon. The bust was like a desert dust storm heading our way. You know it's coming, and there's no way to stop it. The best you can do is to get yourself in a position to hang on when it blows through. In other words, I knew Hungry Minds.com would be a high-wire act; the crash could come at any moment. Even at the beginning, I thought our chances were less than fifty-fifty. If we didn't have money in the bank and a healthy long-term business plan when the crash happened, we'd be dead in the water.

Hungry Minds.com never stood a chance. Because of the impending bust, I rushed the launch of a Web site without thinking through all of the business implications. But it was precisely because of the looming crash that I should have made sure I was on solid ground. Had I taken the time to research online learning, I would have discovered what eventually became clear: the world wasn't yet ready for a complex and extensive online learning portal.

But I didn't want to wait. I figured I would be ninety years old before another speculative bubble where big ideas like Reel.com could happen so fast came along. Here was my chance to do something important, to make the world a better place. I could picture my father telling me as a child that I needed to help others when I grew up because we had the good fortune to be wealthy.

I was going to fulfill that mission.

The Only "B" That Counts: Your Business Plan

Today online learning and training is big business. Many people get graduate degrees with the help of online courses. The University of Phoenix, for example, is a successful Web-based university.

In 1999, however, the online learning industry was in its early phases. There were few courses available and even fewer students to take advantage of them. An industry with a small offering that serves a small market hardly needs a sophisticated portal able to link worldwide resources to a worldwide market.

But the market's enthusiasm for anything dot-com fed my inflated ego. Investors were throwing money at half-baked business ideas. Today I wouldn't be able to raise a dime for Hungry Minds.com. But at the height of the dot-com boom, anything was possible.

I rented a big office south of Market Street in downtown San Francisco and started hiring. Besides marketing, human resource, and other traditional professionals needed for any start-up, I hired twenty high-tech programmers and Web site developers and more than thirty content developers. These would be the writers and editors who would create the course descriptions and other content for the site.

Although I had an eighty-member staff, our success wasn't dependent only on what we could achieve in our San Francisco office. The success of Hungry Minds.com as a portal and reseller also depended on the quality of the content we were reselling. And in the early years of online learning, the quality (not to mention the quantity) wasn't there.

Making the Web fun and interactive takes a lot of money. Producing a good online course costs nearly as much as filming a small movie. You need writers, editors, actors, and producers. A few companies tried to develop inexpensive courseware, but it didn't sell because the quality was so poor.

To overcome the problems with our educational partners, we tried to create classes ourselves—an unrealistic ambition for a small company. Recouping our expenses would have been impossible. In the end, we were limited to selling what was available from others.

Quality and quantity of content weren't our only problems. Even the core idea of our business model—to be a middleman between the creators of education material and the market—was flawed. Online universities sold (and still sell) most of their courses directly to their students. Nobody needed a portal or store like Hungry Minds.com to sell their courseware.

And yet we managed to create a decent brand. During its short life, cover stories in all the education magazines featured Hungry Minds.com. Our site was known as the place to go for education on the Internet. The company had good buzz. But ultimately buzz couldn't save us. We needed a solid business plan, and I didn't have one.

If there's one lesson to take away from Hungry Minds.com, it is this: you can have or build a famous brand and you can create all the great buzz you want, but you will still fail if you haven't nailed down the only "b" that counts: the business plan.

The Crash Roars Closer

One day in 2000, near the pinnacle of the dot-com boom, I ran into two telephone repairmen fixing the phone system at Hungry Minds.com. They had huge smiles on their faces. You could tell the Internet bubble was padding their wallets. I walked up to them and asked, "How do you like this Internet boom?"

They smiled at each other and said, "We love it."

"What do you like the most about it?" I asked.

With a guilty look, one guy sheepishly said, "Internet companies don't ask us about our prices."

These two guys were charging whatever they wanted because people at Internet companies were moving too fast to ask about hourly rates. It's common business knowledge that whenever a business isn't concerned about costs, it can't survive. That's the moment when I felt certain the bust was right around the corner. I would sell Hungry Minds.com at a huge loss less than one month later.

Fail Like a Winner

In June 2000, I sold Hungry Minds.com to IDG Books. In the end, I sold the only thing I had created: a brand. Hungry Minds .com would become the IDG subsidiary for its hugely popular *For Dummies* books. But the massive online learning portal we envisioned was never created by anyone. It's still not a good idea.

Failure is no fun. Hungry Minds.com lasted one year and lost $20 million. Half of that was my money; the rest belonged to my investors, most of them my friends. I felt bad about my friends but worse about my employees. Most of my friends had enough money in the bank to absorb the loss, but many of my employees had left lucrative jobs to work for me. They were the most talented group of people I've ever worked with. When I sold Hungry Minds.com, I gave everyone who stayed with IDG Books six months extra salary as an incentive to stay with the new company and as a thank-you from me.

I also avoided bankruptcy, which was no easy feat. I was ready to shell out a couple of million dollars of my own money to ensure all our creditors were paid. Thankfully, as part of the deal, IDG Books agreed to pay off most of our debt.

There are big lessons here for optimists like me. Once every forty years, you might get lucky like I did with Reel.com. Otherwise, watch out. I had no excuse plunging into the online learning industry without a plan or even a background in the education industry. In the end, I got what I deserved.

CREATE A SECOND BOTTOM LINE FOR YOUR IDEALISM

Many entrepreneurs are idealists. They want to give back to society by creating products or services that improve people's lives. Some prioritize being socially responsible; others contribute to charities. Either way, entrepreneurs need to be businesspeople first and do-gooders second. Strike this balance by creating a "double bottom line" for your company. The first one records your profits; the second one deducts costs incurred by your idealism. Some expenses are obvious, such as contributions to charity. Others are more subtle. For example, when I fire someone, I often give that person extra severance pay (say, four weeks instead of two). I figure that to be fired is traumatic. I want to assuage any feelings of rejection and help keep people afloat until they land another job. In cases such as this, I put the first two weeks of severance pay on the first bottom line and the extra two weeks (costs incurred by my idealism) on the second bottom line. By pinpointing the dollar amount of idealism, the double bottom line helps to adjust those costs when necessary. If your first bottom line suffers—if for whatever reason your profits plunge—you must reduce the extra costs illuminated by the second bottom line. In the end, your going out of business won't help anybody.

CHAPTER 11

Adventures in the Wild

The sharks of the South Pacific are as dangerous as the ones in Silicon Valley.

I was long overdue for a hiatus. I usually give myself at least six months off between start-ups, but the past few years had been a once-in-a-lifetime opportunity. Wanting to squeeze in another Internet business before the big crash, I went from selling Reel.com to starting Hungry Minds.com without much of a break. After I sold Hungry Minds.com, I knew it was time for a vacation.

When I'm not working seventy hours a week on my latest start-up, I'm searching for outdoor thrills. My wife and I love wilderness hiking, long-distance swimming, and spending time around wild animals. We are equally drawn to mountain peaks and remote islands. We were in an enviable position: we had all the money we needed to live out the rest of our lives in comfort. With money as a nonissue, we decided to travel full time. Our dream was to explore the wildest oceans and most remote mountains in the world. We spent a year planning, researching, and scouting our big adventure before embarking on an open-ended vacation. We didn't know if it would last five months or five years, but we did know we wanted it to be the trip of a lifetime.

Whales, Dolphins, or Extraterrestrials?

Our first big adventure was in the South Pacific. We traveled to a remote island and hired a husband and wife team—Mario and Helga—to be our guides. One day we were out looking for wildlife when we met a fisherman who told Mario he'd been deep-sea fishing earlier that day and seen dozens of huge sleeping dolphins.

Upon hearing this news, Mario started shouting, "The melon heads are here! The melon heads are here!" We thought he'd gone off the deep end. What the heck were melon heads? Once he calmed down, he told us that he and Helga were helping marine biologists count the elusive melon-headed whales that frequented the area. Similar in size to large dolphins, melon-headed whales are rarely seen by people because they prefer the deep sea to the shore. Mario and Helga needed to drop everything and go find them. They asked if we were interested in tagging along. Diana and I jumped at the chance to see these unusual animals up close, and before we knew it, we were gunning out to sea in a twenty-four-foot motorboat.

Mario followed the fisherman's directions as best he could, but we didn't see anything. After what seemed like forever, we were all getting hot and tired. Even Mario was losing steam. Then, just when we were about to turn back, we saw what appeared to be dozens of small logs floating in the distance. Mario's face lit up. He slowed the boat and gently steered us toward the logjam. Sure enough, the grouping wasn't logs at all; it was a pod of sleeping melon-headed whales.

Not wanting to disturb them, Mario cut the engine and we paddled closer, careful to keep a respectful distance. For the next three hours, we drifted alongside the dozing animals and took a careful head count. The melon-headed whales are the size of large bottlenose dolphins (adults weigh nearly four hundred pounds) and have an other-worldly energy. They are usually classified as dolphins, but they look and act like whales. I felt as if I was among extraterrestrials. When they weren't snoozing, they were checking us out with an identical sense of wonder. Mario guessed that they had never been near people before. The job was tedious, but what a great feeling to contribute to the scientific understanding of such a magnificent animal. We counted 211 melon-headed whales that afternoon.

Just as we were packing up, we heard a splash from behind the boat and swiveled to see two melon-headed whales swimming playfully at arm's length. Mario explained that when a pod sleeps, a couple of members keep watch. He laughed and said they'd probably been spying on us the entire time. We were so distracted counting that we hadn't even noticed. When Mario revved up the motor and began to coast away from the pod, the watchers escorted us for several miles, playfully jumping in and out of our wake the entire way.

Sea Snakes, Tiger Sharks, and Other Fun Animals

One of our favorite South Pacific destinations is an island so remote it's hard to access even by boat. Surrounded by cliffs, the island has no natural harbors. The only way locals can fish is to lower their boats down the side of a cliff with a crane. Visitors can reach the island only by plane, and just one flight a week lands at the local airport. Miss it, and you've earned yourself a one-week layover. Those who don't have friends or family on the island have one choice of accommodations: a tiny motel. And if you can't sleep in the tropics without air-conditioning, you're limited to the two rooms in the motel with air-conditioning. Organizing the details of a trip like this can take weeks, but it's well worth the trouble.

During one memorable day trip, our guide was an eighty-year-old fisherman named Ernie. He kept a little motorboat in his garage, and when he wanted to take it out, he put it on a trailer, hitched it to a tractor, and towed it to the crane. Diana and I met him at his house early one morning for a day of snorkeling. After introducing ourselves, he jumped on the tractor and waved us into the boat. We hesitated but, after realizing it was ride in the boat or walk, we quickly scrambled into the hull. Ernie proceeded to drive us toward the crane, a route that involved going through the middle of town. I'll never forget the amused looks we got as the islanders stopped to wave. There we were rolling down the street in the boat, as if on a float in the Macy's Thanksgiving Day Parade. As if our impromptu parade wasn't enough excitement for one day, when we arrived at the crane, Diana and I looked at Ernie's feeble arms, checked out the heavy equipment, and summed up that we would be responsible for hand-cranking the crane and lowering the boat fifty feet into the water.

But once we maneuvered ourselves and the boat into the water, Ernie proved to be invaluable. He was an expert in spotting and identifying the local wildlife, including turtles, dolphins, and snakes. We were eager to get into the water for a closer look at some giant turtles when we looked down and saw thousands of sea snakes swarming below the boat. Common in the warm waters of the tropics, sea snakes are one of the most poisonous creatures in the world. "Dive in," said Ernie with a shrug of his bony shoulders. "They won't bite." I stared at the water dubiously. The swarm of sea snakes was so dense the water had turned from blue to orange. But I trusted Ernie implicitly. I gulped some air and jumped in. He was right. Diving into a mass of snakes was strange, but it wasn't life threatening. Neither Diana nor I was bitten. We found out later that sea snakes' mouths are too small to bite people.

Unfortunately, there are plenty of mouths in the sea that aren't too small to bite people. One day while snorkeling in the South Pacific, Diana and I noticed a tiger shark in the distance. This wasn't the first time we'd encountered sharks while snorkeling in the South Pacific, and we weren't worried. The clarity of the water and the sharpness of the knives we had in sheaths strapped to our legs boosted our confidence. But we weren't naive, and we kept an eye on the shark as we continued to enjoy the underwater scenery. As the minutes passed, however, the shark swam closer and what had appeared to be a baby was really a fifteen-foot tiger shark. Now we were worried. In unison, Diana and I began inching toward the boat.

By now the shark was circling us. With each rotation, his loops tightened. As the shark inched closer, Diana let out a scream. At first I thought she was just scared, but when I followed her gaze, I saw what looked like two silver torpedoes coming our way. As they whizzed past us, I saw they were dolphins. Like two heat-seeking missiles, they smashed head first into the shark. BANG! All we could see was a flash of fins and a cloud of sand. When the dust cleared, the shark was nowhere to be seen. The dolphins wheeled around, gave us an "Everybody okay here?" look, and swam off. I'd like to think we would have made it out of that scrape without their help, but they may have saved our lives.

Religious Fanatics Ruin Our Mountain Paradise

For our high-altitude adventures, we'd often rent a camper and head for remote peaks in New Zealand or the American Rockies. Our most memorable mountain adventure was on Evans Lake in British Columbia. A remote five-mile lake cradled in the mountains, Evans Lake is forty miles from civilization and accessible only by floatplane (or so we thought). We hired a pilot who dropped us off near the lake's lone cabin with nothing but our camping gear, food, and a satellite phone so we could call when we were ready to be picked up. The cabin proved to be as primitive as the location, with nothing more than a couple of cots and a small wood stove. Still, we felt as if we'd been dropped in the middle of paradise.

On the second day, it started to rain. After a full day of steady rainfall, I heard what sounded like a continuous thunderclap. The earth-rattling noise went on and on. I asked Diana if she heard it too. She said, "Stuart, I don't think that's thunder." We looked at each other and ran outside just in time to see an avalanche level the side of a nearby mountain. We stood awestruck at the destructive force of Mother Nature. If our cabin had been on the opposite side of the lake, we might have been buried alive.

The next day, I was strolling along the shore when I saw something in the distance. It looked like a raft. But it couldn't be, I thought, taking a harder look. How could it be a raft? I called Diana over, and we watched as the object slowly grew closer. (This was a really big lake.) Sure enough, it was a homemade raft with five men onboard—one lying down and four paddling like fiends.

When they finally landed on our narrow beach, they told us their eldest member was suffering from exposure and needed help. We took them inside the cabin and put the sick man in our bed. We heated up the stove and offered them food and water. As their panic ebbed, their story emerged. They were on a three-month cross-country wilderness trek, and they got more than they bargained for. The last four days of cold rain had been especially tough. They'd eaten nothing but trout and berries for a week. To cross the lake, they'd built the raft from saplings and vines, but they'd overestimated their endurance, and all of them were weak from the effort. Able to see our cabin from miles away, they'd been looking forward to its warmth and comfort for days.

Seven people filled the cabin beyond capacity, so Diana and I grabbed our tent and camped outside. Over the next couple of days, with enough food and rest, the men regained their strength, and Diana and I considered our options. We were happy to help, but we were feeling more than crowded. The thick underbrush meant we had to keep our tent within ten feet of the cabin and therefore within easy conversing distance with our guests. That wouldn't have been a problem except that they were Jehovah's Witnesses. With their energy renewed, they channeled it into trying to convert my wife and me. So there we were, trapped on one of the most remote lakes in North America with five fanatical Jehovah's Witnesses. So much for paradise. Within forty-eight hours, we'd grabbed the satellite phone, called the bush pilot, and begged to be picked up.

Adventures with Captain Bob

Overall we spent eighteen months on vacation. Instead of one long, extended trip, we strung several smaller ones together and spent periods of downtime at our home in San Francisco. We still laugh and reminisce about the people we met and spectacles we saw. The highlight of that year and a half, however, was sharing our happiness and love of adventure with our loved ones. We rented a seventy-foot yacht and over eight weeks took several groups of friends and family members on oceanic adventures. In the end, forty people joined the fun.

Ours wasn't just any old yacht; that it had once belonged to the singer Celine Dion added a whimsical bit of celebrity flair to the occasion. We had everything we needed, including three cabins, three heads, and a souped-up engine. But since most of our friends weren't seaworthy, we mostly slept in hotels on shore.

The trip's highlight was our guide for the summer, Captain Bob. A fifty-five-year-old fisherman who wore his purple heart from the Vietnam War on his lapel, Captain Bob was the saltiest seaman you'd ever hope to meet. On a clear day, he could spot a fin rise above the ocean's surface three miles away and identify the fish. But he never joined us in our underwater sightseeing. No amount of pleading could convince him to get in the water. He kept him saying, "No, I'm just the captain." On the last day, we insisted he try snorkeling. Finally he acquiesced, but before he would get wet, he insisted we tie a rope to the boat's railing and lower it from the back end. When we asked why, he cast his eyes down and mumbled, "I can't swim." We were speechless. Here we'd depended on Captain Bob all summer to ensure our safety on the water and the guy couldn't even swim.

Not long after our return, my wife became ill with a mysterious illness. The best doctors in San Francisco couldn't figure out what was wrong. After months of tests, she was finally diagnosed with chronic Lyme disease. Bedridden for the next three years, she is just now beginning to feel like herself.

Although the past few years have been difficult for both of us, we know how lucky we are. Our trips give us a wonderful shared history that we'll always treasure. We don't know if we'll ever have adventures like those again, but it doesn't matter because we are so full.

CHAPTER 12

Taming a Wild Elephant

I thought I was ready for the biggest project of my life; now I'm not so sure.

I've spent my life turning new ideas into businesses, and for the most part, I've been successful. With the exception of Hungry Minds.com, I've combined my entrepreneurial passions and skills to create cutting-edge enterprises that push the boundaries of their industries. But like Captain Ahab chasing Moby Dick, I became obsessed with a giant of an idea—one that would threaten to destroy my fortune just as I was nearing retirement. Only it wasn't a great white whale that almost did me in—it was an elephant.

The Vision

The idea, which became an obsession, was to create a giant holistic pharmacy by combining the medical traditions of the West and the East in a one-stop-shopping experience. I envisioned Elephant as the only pharmacy in the country with two full-service pharmacies: one for prescriptions and one for herbs. My dream was seeing customers' shopping bags filled with aspirin and echinacea, ear candles and Q-tips.

I also wanted to feel good about what we didn't carry: chemical-infused beauty products, junk food, and tobacco. To that end, I wanted to build the largest all-natural cosmetics and body care department in the world. Customers could make appointments with estheticians who used only 100 percent natural beauty products for makeovers and facials. Instead of the unhealthy snacks found at other drugstores, my food department would contain only natural and organic offerings.

The main reason Elephant Pharmacy appealed to me wasn't the concept of Eastern medicine meeting Western medicine, though I have long been a believer in alternative remedies; my biggest motivation and inspiration was customer education. Here I saw an opportunity to take my movie-matchmaking expertise to a whole new industry. I envisioned a revolutionary store that would not only have a unique product mix from around the world but also be the first big-box retail concept focused on education. Customer education would differentiate my business from the competition, just as it had at Empire and Reel.com.

My vision wasn't just a pipe dream. I created it. You can shop at Elephant Pharmacy in Berkeley and visit its sister store in San Rafael. You'll find the stores as I've described them above. But as I drive by them today, I know that the cost of turning my vision into reality was too high for me. This was one adventure I should have passed up.

Love Is Blind

It all started in 2001 when I fell in love with my new business idea. It consumed me day and night. My mind raced with thoughts of how I'd create the perfect store: educational materials built into the shelves, free classes for the community, and free consultations with alternative health practitioners. I got so excited I'd wake up Diana in the middle of the night to share my latest brainstorm.

When you start a business, you need to foresee the potential problems, not just the good things. My passion gave me the zeal to make things happen, but it also blinded me. I have enough gray hair to know how much trouble I can get into when I let my emotions guide my decisions. But Elephant was a seductive idea for this idealistic baby boomer entrepreneur.

The Spark That Started the Great Fire

The concept of Elephant Pharmacy didn't appear out of nowhere. I'd thought about the idea for a long time. Anthony Harnett and I had talked about it often when I was at Bread & Circus. Twelve years ago, I helped him start a similar business, Harnett's Apothecary, in Harvard Square. An alternative pharmacy, Harnett's Apothecary sold natural remedies and body care products but didn't delve into prescription drugs.

If Harnett's Apothecary was the kindling, the spark was an innovative chain of pharmacies in Colorado called Pharmaca. Pharmaca was converting small neighborhood pharmacies into stores that sold both Eastern and Western medicines. At Pharmaca you could pick up your antibiotic prescription as well as Oregon Grapefruit Extract for that sore throat. As soon as I heard about Pharmaca filling prescriptions, a bell went off. I said, "Of course. Everyone I know is getting older. We all love the idea of alternative medicine, but we are also on Lipitor. Putting Eastern medicine and Western prescriptions under the same roof would create the perfect pharmacy for people like me who shop at Whole Foods."

For eighteen months, I'd been traveling around the world with Diana, swimming and snorkeling in the wildest oceans on earth. I was having the time of my life in semiretirement. I had all the money I needed and the woman of my dreams. I was happy. I returned to San Francisco and thought about consulting a little, but I wasn't looking for a new project. I was having too much fun.

Nevertheless, fueled by my passion for education, my retail experience with natural products, and my constant desire to invent radical new businesses, the spark became a raging bonfire that would eventually burn through most of my fortune.

An Elephant Can't Be Small

I went to Colorado to check out Pharmaca for myself. The stores were cool, but their diminutive size was a turn-off. I like big stores, called "category killers," that make a big impression on people and on the marketplace. The array of products, services, and information I envisioned wouldn't have fit into Pharmaca's footprint. These small stores rarely have an impact beyond their upscale neighborhoods. They just preach to the converted. I wanted to have an impact on millions, which meant I needed a BIG store.

The other reason I wanted a big-box store was to have great customer service. Sure, small stores have the best service if it's a mom-and-pop business because of the pride of ownership. But if your company needs to be a chain, large stores can offer much better and more personal service than small stores. The big difference is that in a large store, you can pay management a lot more money. A typical drugstore chain might pay store managers $40,000 per year. At Elephant, we planned to pay $100,000, which means we could afford much more talented managers. Since the store manager is responsible for hiring, training, and motivating the staff, better management means happier and better-trained employees.

When I told the Pharmaca people about my big-box idea, they weren't interested. They were content with their less complicated business model. I should have considered that a red flag, but I was blinded by my passion. So I determined to bring

Elephant Pharmacy to life by myself. On December 7, 2001, I decided to turn my vision into reality.

The Right Man for the Job (or So I Thought)

I was the perfect person to start Elephant Pharmacy. I'd spent most of my career marketing to baby boomers, from the James Montgomery Band in the 1970s to environmental issues and natural foods in the 1980s. I'd learned retail operations while working for Bread & Circus. I invented education-focused business models at Empire Video and Reel.com. And I knew the ins and outs of high-end retail real estate. I had plenty of money to bankroll the project (or so I thought). And, last but not least, I practice what I preach by eating organic foods, doing yoga, and meditating.

Start on the Right Foot

The first step in organizing any business is to put your start-up team together. Elephant's first employee was Sandy Sickley, who'd been with me at Empire Video, Reel.com, and Hungry Minds.com. Together we hired Minda Lehto, from Reel.com, to be our content editor, and Susie Larson, from Hungry Minds.com, as an administrative assistant. We set up a small office in San Francisco and began to turn my vision of Elephant into a reality.

The task was daunting. We were simultaneously starting a complicated company and creating a new business model. We needed a name, brand, logo, product mix, business plan, store design, real estate, and a marketing plan. Above all else, I wanted Elephant to educate customers to make healthful choices, so I invested large sums to create wellness information for distribution throughout the store. We hired as many writers and editors during those early days as we did retailers. We even invented our own pullout system to display information below the products. I approached the holistic pharmacy business the same way I approached movie matchmaking and found that helping people to find the right remedy was just as exciting as helping them to discover a new film they'd enjoy. Here, though, the challenge was infinitely greater because we were dealing with people's health.

After putting the executive team together, the next two steps were finding our first store location and hiring a CEO. Unfortunately, just as these decisions were being made, I became sick. The timing could not have been worse.

When it comes to the fate of a business, I put a lot of stock in luck, both good and bad. Just when things got rolling—architects, real estate brokers, and headhunters were all on board—I was laid up for two months with kidney stones. While I was lying in bed writhing in pain, everything I had put into motion over the past three months started to go wrong. I made two big mistakes in particular that would prove very expensive.

Fail to the Chief

I made my first big mistake when I hired our CEO. I wanted to design and create the business but did not want to run the company. My management skills are not a good fit for Elephant's complexity. So within the first two months, I went looking for an experienced executive.

After an exhaustive search, I thought I'd found a great candidate—a superstar retailer who was the general manager for all of retail at Nike. Best of all, she was passionate about herbs and loved the idea of Elephant. After two three-hour interviews, we hired her.

I was in agony with my kidney stones and heavily medicated both times we met. She couldn't have gotten a more misleading impression of me. Because of the painkillers, I was slow, mellow, and relaxed. Normally I am fast-talking, hyperactive, and extremely intense. Neither one of us was thinking clearly because I offered her the job, and she accepted it. As it turned out, we had just embarked on a bad marriage. She was a brilliant big-company chief operating officer, great at managing a large number of people in a structured environment. But Elephant was a small, chaotic start-up, and she was a fish out of water.

We parted ways after she spent only four months on the job, just two months before the launch of our first store. The change in management threw the company off-kilter and put a damper on what should have been one of the happiest days of my life: the opening of the first Elephant Pharmacy. Later she told me that if I had been my normal self during those meetings, she would have turned down the job because she would have known that our personalities wouldn't mesh. Since one of her talents is reading people, I believe her.

Location, Location, Location

My second mistake was choosing the wrong location. Although I had a good track record picking store locations, this was a particularly difficult decision. The Elephant concept was so untested we didn't even know what kind of real estate we needed: a neighborhood location, like other drugstores, or a regional location, like Nordstrom. And our options in the Bay Area were limited. Berkeley was the only place we could find the real estate we needed: a large building with plenty of parking in an upscale neighborhood. The building didn't come cheap. Just to negotiate a lease, I had to pay $1 million in cash on top of our exorbitant rent for the privilege of renting the spot.

In some ways, a Berkeley store appealed to me. The city's residents are a wonderful group to try out a new concept on because they don't hesitate to tell you what they think. But in other ways, our location was all wrong. For starters, Berkeley residents don't like chains. We were in an isolated neighborhood, far off the freeway, surrounded by healthy, young university students. An upscale drugstore is the last place healthy, budget-conscious students are going to spend a lot of money. We needed a larger population of older, affluent people who are either working to stay healthy or managing multiple chronic diseases. Those young folks in Berkeley didn't even need our natural cosmetics because they were all so attractive.

Opening Day Disaster: Let's Make a Deal!

When the store opened on November 25, 2002, we weren't ready. Although the construction was done and the shelves were stocked, there was one important thing missing: the computer system. I had great techies (for once), but they didn't understand retailing, which created unexpected delays in the rollout of the system. To make matters worse, we had brought together a large worldwide mix of wholesalers and suppliers, but none of them had worked together before. As a result, the majority of the store's twenty-five thousand products weren't priced. But I didn't care. I was tired of waiting. I wanted to open the store so I could finally get customers' feedback.

What a disaster! The store's atmosphere was reminiscent of the classic game show *Let's Make a Deal.* Customers would ask the price of an item, and the cashier would say, "What do you think it's worth?" It took three months to straighten out the glitches and price the merchandise.

Compounding our problems, we opened in the middle of the holiday season. November and December are the worst time to open because people are too busy to think about switching to a new drugstore. In addition, they are inundated with so much advertising from established stores that a new store gets lost in the shuffle. Holidays are the only time shoppers aren't interested in the words *grand opening.*

The Good News: Competitors Pay Attention

Even with our mishaps, the drugstore industry couldn't get enough of us. The first eight customers standing in line on the day we opened were Walgreens managers. We opened an hour late that morning. They waited. Later the chain's district manager told me, "We would have waited all day because this is the first new concept in the drugstore business in fifty years." In the following months, so many executives from drugstores around the world descended on Elephant Pharmacy that the staff joked about needing to put a limo stop out front. Our employees called them "the suits" because they stood out like sore thumbs in Birkenstock Berkeley.

As of the writing of this book, many companies are taking lessons from Elephant. Best Buy has opened its third big upscale pharmacy, which is similar to Elephant Pharmacy. Located in Minnesota, it's called eq-life. Longs imitated us by putting class-rooms in some of its stores. Rite Aid is forming partnerships with Wild Oats. And The Limited bought New York's Bigalows Chemists and is retooling it into a chain of natural skin care stores. Even Pharmaca is copying us. Its newest store, in Santa Fe, New Mexico, is very much like Elephant Pharmacy.

Changing Everything; Then Changing Everything Again!

The industry attention was gratifying, but our finances were a disaster. Within weeks of opening, I could see Elephant Pharmacy was in big trouble. The store was losing more than fifty thousand dollars a week, and changes we made added to the expense. Some changes were to be expected; you never get it right the first time on a project so big and new. But instead of being the end of a job well done, the opening was just the beginning.

Here are some of the most expensive changes we made to the store in the first few months based on customer feedback:

- We started out shelving many Eastern and Western medi-cines together, but our customers quickly made it clear they wanted them separate. So we reorganized the herb, supple-ments, and over-the-counter drug sections even though it meant moving more than seventy thousand products.

- At first, all books were in our bookstore at the back of the store. But we decided customers should have access to them while they shopped, so we designed and built book-shelves to sit on top of the shelves throughout the store. The books helped sell the products sitting below and also spread the message that we were serious about education.

We also expanded our bookstore to include three thousand titles.

- Neighborhood customers requested high-quality food. In response, we tore apart the store to add a prep room, a walk-in refrigerator, and plumbing for refrigerated displays. In the end, we had a large, fresh organic produce and food department. Our fruits and vegetables were 99 percent organic, which made us stand out even in Berkeley.

- We didn't expect the classes to be so popular. In the beginning, we squeezed students into the bookstore, but the crowds outgrew the space. So we expanded our offerings, cut back our stationery department, and used the space to build a classroom with a capacity of fifty. Local practitioners began offering as many as six free classes a day.

- We reorganized the stationery department several times. Originally the section was huge. We had a whole wall just for pens. Eventually the greeting card section shrank to one-fourth its original size, and the pen wall was eliminated.

- We expanded our program of free advice from practitioners to seven days a week, adding a desk in front of the consultation room so that customers could get professional advice while they shopped.

Berkeley in Love

Winning over the community was tough. Our biggest challenge was convincing them that Elephant wasn't just another big-box chain store, which can be synonymous with poor service, bad selection, and unhealthy food. The turning point came in March. The store was finally coming together. Computer systems were up and running, and our employees were delivering top-notch customer service. Our merchandise mix was almost complete, and the store no longer looked like a construction site.

We were finally ready to do some serious business. Now we had to figure out how to tell people that Elephant wasn't Walgreens. After many unsuccessful experiments, we finally hit on how best to spread the word about Elephant: a massive customer education promotion. We mailed an eight-page course catalogue to fifty thousand households in the area and distributed it everywhere we could think of. Bicycle messengers delivered them to local doctor's offices, yoga studios, stores, and restaurants. We even hired students to distribute the catalogues at subway stops during rush hour. Since our free classes were a great community service, it was easy to get the word out. Spending all that money on promoting education was scary, but we had a lot of evidence from customer suggestions and focus groups that wellness education would get people's attention. My favorite quote from the focus groups came from a busy lawyer: "I'm not sure if I will ever have time to take any of your free classes, but I will be sure to shop in your store because you offer them."

The response to our course catalogue was tremendous. Baby boomers showed up at the store by the hundreds with catalogues in hand and suspicious looks on their faces. They were still cynical about this new drugstore, but free wellness classes and our latest tagline—The Drugstore That Thinks It's a University—piqued their curiosity.

I spent many happy hours hanging out in the store that March, watching skeptical new customers become Elephant believers. Their dubious expressions gradually changed to smiles, then really big smiles, as they walked through the store. Between the organic produce, the huge natural cosmetic section, and the friendly, knowledgeable staff, they could see our store was nothing like the typical chain drugstore. It was much healthier and, at least for most people, a lot more fun. Rather than listening to Musak, they heard Bob Dylan and Buffalo Springfield. Even the way our store smelled was different. We had a variety of soothing aromas from our fresh flowers, natural soaps, herbal teas, and incense.

On surveys, more than 75 percent of our customers rated Elephant as their favorite or second-favorite shopping destination (not favorite drugstore—favorite *store*). The customers grew to love Elephant so much that they brought me thank-you gifts. I soon had two copies of *Zen Judaism* as well as an expensive Zen alarm clock and a hand-knit scarf. I took the gifts as a sign the community appreciated our vision and our blood, sweat, and tears. But the greatest gift of all was the increase in sales. That month began a period of explosive sales growth.

Not Out of the Woods . . .

As the months passed and the store headed toward profitability, we enjoyed many successes. But even with customers crowding the store, money and time were running out. Our cost structure was too high for a single store; we needed revenues from multiple stores to cover marketing and overhead expenses, such as ad campaigns and executive salaries. The unusual and diverse combination of products and services we offered and the slow growth in sales and customers inherent in the pharmacy industry added to the extraordinary start-up costs.

As a result of these cost pressures, Elephant was bleeding me dry. Although the business was starting to look very promising, there were still plenty of risks. I had to choose between using my retirement money to keep the company going or selling the store. With the wisdom of hindsight, I should have walked away, but I couldn't bring myself to do it. I couldn't disappoint all of our enthusiastic customers, so I continued to raid my retirement accounts and tried to raise more money.

We hired great investment bankers and talked to dozens of potential investors. We contacted anyone who might share our vision or want to capitalize on it, from venture capitalists to trust fund hippies. At first glance, investors loved us because of the phenomenal success of similar big-box stores like Whole Foods. But when they looked at our numbers, they told us to call them back when the store became profitable.

Eventually, in October 2003, I found two potential investors: JP Morgan and CVS Pharmacy. The key player was CVS. When I called Chris Bodine, CVS's second in command, I knew he was my best hope. Through the grapevine, I'd been told he was the only executive in the pharmacy industry who believed in wellness, customer education, and natural products. Setting up a meeting with him was easy, which made me optimistic, but I was unsettled when we were finally face-to-face. We'd hardly finished shaking hands when he began to grill me. "Why did you move your floral department again?" he asked, "I can't figure out why you keep moving it." The fact that he knew where our flowers were shocked me. CVS headquarters is in Woonsocket, Rhode Island, about as far away from Berkeley as you can get. As it turned out, they'd been watching us closely for months. After I explained my decision to move the flowers, Chris gave me a big smile. "Congratulations on Elephant," he said. "You guys have created something we never could have done."

Note to the reader: Just before I completed this book I signed a legal document that restricts me from writing about events at Elephant after October 31, 2003.

Don't Underestimate the Challenges: A Guidebook for Entrepreneurs

When I first planned Elephant Pharmacy, everyone said it was the best idea they'd ever heard. The baby boomer generation needs a holistic drug store, they said. Look at the success of Whole Foods. But their enthusiasm made me nervous. If this idea is so brilliant, why hadn't somebody else tried it? I wasn't the only entrepreneur who could see that the Whole Foods' customers were aging and would need a drugstore. The big lesson here is that if an idea is obvious but nobody else has tried it, there is probably a good reason. The reason nobody had invented an elephant-type pharmacy is that it's too expensive for one person to pioneer and too original for a big company to create. The concept had to wait for a creative guy, like me, who was willing to spend a lot of money.

I hoped a partnership with a big company would help us overcome our remaining challenges: being so unique and being too small to compete.

Below are some of the unusual issues I faced at Elephant.

The Model

The biggest problem at first was our innovative business model. The drugstore industry is brutal. Big health maintenance organizations (HMOs) have squeezed the profits out of the prescription business. We discovered the hard way that one reason no one else ever opened a big-box upscale pharmacy is that these stores, which are driven by prescription sales, ramp—or grow—slowly because people are slow to switch pharmacies. That accounted for half of the outrageous losses we incurred when we launched our operation, which was much more expensive to operate than the traditional pharmacy. We needed to modify the slow-ramping pharmacy model by aggressively promoting education so customers would come in faster and reduce our early losses. We also promoted the other departments in our store to move away from the prescription-driven business model.

Purchasing

Because our chain store competitors bought items in such huge quantities, they paid about 10 percent less for their inventory than we did. To compound the problem, everything from ad space to store supplies was more expensive on a small scale.

Stocking Elephant was a challenge because it was a complicated one-of-a-kind business. Our product mix had never been sold under the same roof before, so we sourced inventory from seven hundred suppliers instead of just one, like most other drugstores do. Because of the complexity of its inventory, Elephant should have had four buyers, but we could afford only one.

Elephant was so different that even our insurance rates were outrageous. We paid forty thousand dollars extra per year in liability insurance because we distributed our own wellness information.

Technology

Elephant needed to manage twenty-five thousand items and two in-store pharmacies; we needed sophisticated technology to handle that level of complexity. Available off-the-shelf applications didn't work well because our store was both high volume and one-of-a-kind. However, we had no choice. Chain drugstores customize their technology, but we didn't have the money or time to build our own.

Marketing

I underestimated the importance of marketing because I came from the natural supermarket business. Natural supermarkets have six "perishable" departments—bakery, produce, dairy, fish, meats, and deli—that keep customers coming back twice a week. The big draw for a drugstore is prescriptions, which people get filled roughly once a month. That's why you see lots of advertising for Walgreens and very few ads for Whole Foods. Since we had only one store in a major market, we couldn't afford to use the media to advertise. We couldn't even afford a marketing department.

Human Resources

Our biggest hurdle was paying for the corporate infrastructure— a comptroller, education director, tech support, and so forth. In a chain, these positions benefit from economies of scale: you need one chief financial officer (CFO) whether you have one store or ten. Obviously the ratio of CFO salary to revenues is much more reasonable if you have ten stores. We didn't. As a result, we could afford only a part-time CFO, and we skimped by not having a human resource department.

Hiring and training for a new concept like Elephant also presents endless quandaries. For instance, how do we find an education director? Since we created the job description ourselves, there were no résumés coming in that perfectly matched our needs. For each new employee we hired, dozens had to be interviewed. And who will train and supervise the new employee?

Being a "granola company" also posed challenges. Few corporate cultures are similar to Elephant's, which made it hard to find employees with the right skills who also fit into the culture. The problem harkened back to my early days of Bread & Circus.

Real Estate

All start-ups needing prime real estate have a near mission impossible. Landlords of quality real estate are required by their mortgage lenders to pick older, credit-worthy tenants. Property managers often won't even talk to start-ups. Our business model for future stores could not support the $1 million in key money we paid in Berkeley, so we hoped a large company would help us with lease guarantees.

Greener Pastures

Elephant Pharmacy almost ruined me. I eventually sank almost all my money—$13 million—into the start-up. My wife and I aren't as young or as healthy as we used to be. We've been through some difficult years due to the stress caused by both her illness and putting our retirement savings at risk. Although Elephant will probably be very successful, the price was too high. If I were younger and wealthier, it would have been a great project.

That said, I'm proud of my work. With the help of hundreds of dedicated employees and thousands of customers, we invented a new pharmacy business model. Elephant focuses on wellness and keeping people healthy, not just managing disease. Finally, we turned the traditional pharmacy business model upside down. Drugstores like Walgreens generate more than 70 percent of their revenue through prescriptions and over-the-counter drugs. At Elephant, less than 30 percent of our business came from drugs. Elephant sold more products to keep people healthy than it did to cure illness.

Judging by the scores of pharmacy executives who visited Elephant, it is likely to have a big impact on the industry. Drugstore chains like Walgreens may soon have stores that come in two flavors: regular and green.

AVOID CREATIVITY AT ALL COSTS

The key to balancing creativity and entrepreneurship is to borrow as much as you can from others. Don't look for out-of-the-box solutions. Find other people who are either doing what you want to do or doing pieces of your plan. Nothing is so new that someone hasn't already mastered parts of it. There are three reasons to avoid creativity.

Creativity Is Too Expensive

Thinking outside the box takes time and money, both in short supply at most start-ups.

The Wheel Has Already
Been Invented, So Use It

Nine times out of ten, someone has already solved the puzzle you are flummoxed over. At first I questioned whether Walgreens executives were smart to dedicate so much floor space to greeting cards. Once the holidays rolled around, I quickly saw how cards baited shoppers into buying presents too. People went in for a card and came out with both a card and a gift. It was a forehead-slapping moment. Of course, Walgreens knew what worked; it had been perfecting its business practices for seventy-five years.

Half of All Creative Ideas
Are Thrown Out Anyway

I'm a creative person. Some of my ideas are brilliant; others are stinkers. The problem is I don't know which are which until it's all said and done. One of my favorite business lines is from David Ogilvy, the founder of modern advertising. He said that half the money he spends on advertising is completely wasted, but he doesn't know which half. The same goes for creativity. When I am in the middle of a creative project, I know at least half of my ideas are going to be wasted. My only problem is that I don't know which half. Half the time, my creativity can make or break my business because it makes my business special. Creativity is attention getting, but you need to exercise caution. Because creativity is so expensive, you can afford to do only one or two things, so it's important to meet some basic criteria: (1) choose something doable, (2) choose something important, and (3) if you can copy something your competitors did in the past, do.

CHAPTER 13

What It Takes (and Doesn't Take) to Be an Entrepreneur

Know yourself, keep learning, and hang on for the ride!

When you make a mistake in business, any successful entrepreneur will tell you to own it, learn from it, and move on. In other professions, mistakes can be a disaster; surgeons, lawyers, and accountants are paid a premium for perfection. But mistakes are a daily part of life for serial entrepreneurs. I constantly assess risk and minimize failure. I've won some, and I've lost some. I've made mistakes so huge they crippled my company. A start-up is like a house of cards: one blunder, and the entire operation can collapse. Here are some lessons you can learn from my mistakes.

Mixing Business and Revolution Is Dangerous

When you start a business, you need to focus on profit (unless you start a nonprofit). If you prioritize helping people, your attention won't be on making money, and your business will fail. The trick to starting a business that is both sustainable and socially conscious is to pick a model where helping people is profitable.

I've worked hard to strike this balance; sometimes it worked, and other times it didn't. Elephant Pharmacy's customer education component is my favorite example of this win-win principle in action. The classes, advice practitioners, and learning opportunities provide retail theater, sell products, attract customers, foster community outreach, and help people be healthy. Hungry Minds.com was big on revolution but short on profit. I couldn't figure out how to turn online learning into a sustainable business, and the company failed. It was a lose-lose situation. We neither helped people nor recouped our investment.

Slow Down When Necessary

Speed is a boon for some, but for me it can be problematic. I have the attention span of a flea. Each of my mentors has tried to slow me down. Over the years, I've gotten better at stepping on the brakes, but learning how and when to decelerate is still my biggest challenge.

Not slowing down long enough to fly to Europe and solidify the relationship between Reel.com and the Internet Movie Database (IMDb) was costly. The partnership was crucial for Reel.com's future. For four months, I told myself I should visit its London-based headquarters to cement the relationship, but I was too busy. But a fear of slowing down didn't keep Jeff Bezos, founder of Amazon.com, from going. He went to England and bought IMDb right out from under me.

My speed-induced decision to open Elephant Pharmacy before the computer systems were operational was very expensive because the mistake paralyzed the company for at least three months. And that wasn't the only Elephant mistake I attribute to my impatience. When I hired the wrong CEO, my kidney stones kept me from thinking the decision through, but, regardless, two interviews are not enough to judge a CEO candidate. I should have known better.

Over the years, I've learned to slow down by creating structure and imposing discipline. For instance, I have a new rule for filling executive positions: at least three people must interview each candidate once, and two people must interview the candidate twice. I also surround myself with more grounded people. Sandy Sickley has helped me start every business since Empire. She is methodical, deliberate, and very observant—my complete opposite. After I fired Elephant's first CEO, I didn't fill any top positions without Sandy's approval.

Never, Ever Underestimate Technology

I'm afraid of machines. They call for slowing down and being precise, two things that drive me crazy. It doesn't help that I can't spell or type. My fear of all things mechanical is why Scott Beck at Blockbuster had to drag me into the computer age. My weakness goes well beyond speed; it's more like a mental block. Not prioritizing technology at Empire Video cost a fortune. For two years, we couldn't collect late fees, which cut our profits in half. Bumbling the technology at Reel.com was my most expensive mistake ever. In concept, Reel.com was ahead of the curve; if it hadn't been for our inadequate technology, our company could have been another Amazon.com.

Since then I have worked much harder to get the technology right. To that end, I spend a lot more money on technology. Knowing that I have a track record of mismanaging technology helps me compensate. In fact, sometimes I overcompensate. My only technical problem with Hungry Minds.com was that I spent too much money. Afraid of repeating my mistake, I hired the best techies money could buy. But in the end, I wasted both their expertise and my cash because their skills and enthusiasm for bells and whistles far outpaced the company's needs.

Know When to Pull the Plug

In the big-business picture, knowing when to hold 'em and when to fold 'em is of utmost importance. Sometimes a business can be good for the customers but bad for the entrepreneur. An example is Elephant Pharmacy. People love Elephant, but because of my wife's illness and the stress of the financial risk, the business was a mistake.

Let me clarify. I don't consider either starting the business or putting in $6 million to get Elephant off the ground a mistake. My mistake came later. I should have known better when I dumped my last $6 million into Elephant to keep it afloat. I was playing with money I couldn't afford to lose. I risked my retirement money because my ego can't handle failure.

Likewise, in Chapter Seven, I described working on a business design for an educational toy store. I spent six months and roughly $300,000 on real estate brokers, payroll, artwork, consultants, and other experts. Then I killed the project the day we were scheduled to sign our first lease. The odds for success were good, but I wasn't in a good position to start a new company. Walking away from the project was a smart move. Over the past twenty years, I spent a substantial amount of time and money on at least six other projects, only to cut bait before they launched. In addition to the weekly newspaper and fruit soda ideas I mentioned earlier, I dabbled in natural potato chips, ecotourism, medicinal teas, and healthy fast food. I don't consider any of those half-baked ideas mistakes. Entrepreneurs need to try new businesses on for size to see if they are a good fit. Sometimes that's the only way to find out if the business is going to work. If it's not a good fit, do yourself a favor and walk away.

Don't Fly Blind

I took Kit Richert, my assistant, to one of my high-stakes poker games. I wanted to teach her what it was like to fly blind. She was overly anxious to start her own business, and I was trying to slow her down. (Imagine me trying to slow down someone else!) At the end of each hand, I had her guess what the other players' cards were at the table. She was almost always wrong. I pointed to a world-class poker player who was also playing that day who "guessed" right every time. First, she thought he must be cheating. Then she thought he might be psychic. Of course, he was neither. He was just a great poker player. You learn a lot when you play full time for twenty years. All businesses have experienced, knowledgeable players. Inexperienced players rarely win.

The time I blindly flew into a huge mistake was when I started Hungry Minds.com. Driven by arrogance and a windfall from Reel.com, I jumped into the education business, an industry where making a profit is notoriously difficult, without a viable business model. Worst of all, I had never worked in the education industry before.

Empire Video was just the opposite. Video was a new industry, so I knew as much as anybody else. With my movie buff background and my experience with the James Montgomery Band, I knew something about both film and entertainment. Before I jumped in, I spent six months researching video stores. The industry was a perfect fit for my talents in marketing, merchandising, and real estate. In addition, I was comfortable running a small chain in small towns, just like my father and my grandfather had.

Don't Design Your Business Around You

Starting a successful business is unbelievably hard. Everything must go your way if you want to overcome the barriers to success. Just like parenting a newborn, a new start-up demands big lifestyle changes and sacrifices on your part. If you're unwilling to change, your business will be in jeopardy.

When I founded Empire Video, I was so desperate for success that I moved from my comfortable home in Boston to a farmhouse in Vermont without a moment's hesitation. By the time I started Elephant Pharmacy sixteen years later, I was a rich guy buoyed by the security and comfort of my wealth. I was no longer hungry or desperate, two qualities a start-up CEO needs. My wife and I loved living in San Francisco, and I didn't want to uproot myself for my company. So I designed the business around my needs instead of its needs.

I knew my first store needed to be in the country's only sizable upscale market where both real estate and marketing were cheap and simple: Santa Fe, New Mexico. So although Santa Fe was the perfect town to test and perfect my new business model, I stayed in San Francisco because I didn't want to move. The Bay Area was a terrible place to start Elephant Pharmacy for two reasons. First, it's almost impossible for a start-up to lease upscale, big-box real estate. Even after the dot-com bust, San Francisco still had the toughest real estate market in the country. I went across the Bay and opened the first Elephant Pharmacy in a quiet Berkeley neighborhood, a less-than-ideal location, because my choices were so limited.

Another big drawback was marketing. I couldn't afford to advertise in such a big media market. I only had one store. Even established chains in established industries don't enter such big metropolitan markets with fewer than five stores because that's the only way they can afford to advertise.

Be Financeable

You have to convince others that your idea deserves their money and that you're the one to turn that idea into a reality. Part of making yourself financeable is paying your dues: making contacts and building a reputation while learning the ropes.

Paying your dues often means making short-term sacrifices to achieve long-term goals. For instance, I hated the real estate business, but I used it as a stepping-stone. At first, not even the video business appealed to me, but I desperately wanted a big opportunity I could afford with my small bankroll. When I had the idea for the *People's Almanac* at age twenty-five, I wasn't in a position to execute it. I wasn't financeable in the publishing business, so the feasibility of my idea didn't matter.

On the flip side, being financeable doesn't mean you deserve the money. Look at the hundreds of dot-com entrepreneurs who got funded but didn't have the know-how to spend it wisely. When that happens, everyone loses. I deserved financing at Empire Video, but I hadn't proven myself and thus I had a hard time. At Hungry Minds.com, my experience was just the opposite: I easily received millions of dollars to launch a start-up that had a lousy business model.

The Contradictions of an Entrepreneur

Know your strengths and weaknesses. Creativity is my biggest strength. (It's a weakness too.) But that doesn't mean all entrepreneurs need to be creative to be successful. You can buy creativity, you can hire creative people, you can steal creative ideas, and you can even learn to be more creative. Take your pick. It's not important to be creative, but it is important to know if you are creative so you can compensate if you need to.

My friend Scott Beck claims not to be creative, but he has something more valuable: a knack for appreciating creativity in others. He knows a good idea when he sees one. The minute he heard about a little eight-store chain of video stores in Texas called Blockbuster, he saw the potential.

I have hundreds of creative ideas. The trick is figuring out which ones are good. Scott had both the ability to appreciate others' creativity and the self-awareness to see his own strengths and weaknesses. I owe my self-awareness to my mentors: my father, James Montgomery, Anthony Harnett, J.J. on Haight Street, Scott Beck, and others. But the mentor I think about most, even though I've only seen her twice in the past twelve years, is my former psychotherapist, Sonia. She helped me accomplish one of my biggest goals in life, a happy love life, and that has been great for my career too.

Being a successful entrepreneur means embracing contradiction. You must be simultaneously desperate and confident, scared and excited, a risk taker and not a gambler. Ultimately you need to be a clear thinker who is also just a little bit crazy.

HOW TO MAKE THE TRANSITION FROM A BIG COMPANY TO A START-UP

If you've read this book, most likely you dream of becoming an entrepreneur someday. And if you're like most other entrepreneur wannabes, you are biding your time and paying your dues by slaving away at a large but established company. My enthusiasm for adventure can be contagious, but before you take the plunge and submit your resignation, consider the following final pieces of advice:

- Know what you're getting into. You've got to retrain your big-company brain. A start-up is another dimension. Put aside everything you think you know about business, and enter your start-up with an open mind. Being ready for things to look, feel, and sound completely foreign will increase your odds of navigating the rough waters ahead.
- Toss out the rule book. Big companies operate through structure and predictability. Small companies do things on a case-by-case basis. Flexibility is your greatest asset. For instance, the owner of a big business might have a strict "no checks" policy to lower the chances of getting a bad check. But many times small business owners, like those I met while biking cross-country, know the folks in their community well enough to know who can write good checks and who can't.
- Check your motivation. At some point, everyone dreams about being his own boss. Be careful. Hating your job is not by itself a good reason to start a business.
- Start a business on the side. Before you resign from your day job, try self-employment on for size by starting a small business. Any kind of business will do. Do you want to cater parties, paint houses, or walk dogs? Capitalize on your passions.

- Talk to people who've made the transition. Seek out business owners with similar likes, dislikes, and lifestyles. If you're the sole supporter of a large family who likes his weekends and evenings free, don't solicit business advice from a bachelor workaholic entrepreneur. If you look and don't find like-minded people who've made the leap, it might be a sign that the start-up world is not right for you.

- Get a job at a start-up before you start a start-up. You'll learn more by being a part of someone else's adventure than you would on your own. You would learn not just how to do a better start-up, but what your role should be and what your strengths and weaknesses are and maybe even whether you should do the start-up at all. That is the biggest thing you can learn: whether you are making the right decision to do the right thing.

- Be financially prepared. That's something that any decent business book will tell you. Start-ups are always more expensive and more time-consuming than you think. The best way to buttress yourself for the bumps ahead is to have a financial cushion to soften the blows. Add up your planned expenses, and then double them.

Acknowledgments

I am neither a good writer nor a good editor; therefore, I am grateful to my two partners, Catherine Guthrie and Chris Murray. Chris, my editor, and Catherine, my co-writer, not only coaxed forth my stories but also made them sing.

I also received invaluable help from my two assistants: Kit Richert, a brilliant future entrepreneur, and Heather O'Neill, a talented writer with a gift for organizing my thoughts.

Thanks to Neal Maillet and Susan Williams at Jossey-Bass for their vision, insight, and support.

Thanks to Amy Nathan for the original cover idea as well as to Adrian Morgan and Dale Higgins for the final design. Kudos to my transcriber, Andrea Fiore, whose effort went far beyond her job description.

Thanks to Jack Robertson, Elephant's original brand guru, for his brilliant work, including the tagline "The Drug Store That Thinks It's a University."

Thank you Stu-Art and Suzanna for all of your music, especially the song "Easy Dot Com, Easy Dot Go."

Several people have been influential in my life but don't play large roles in the book, so I want to be sure to thank them. These include my best friends, Marv, Richard, Anthony, and Dick, and two great psychotherapists, Rodger and Chris.

And, always, a thank you to my wife, Diana, my partner in life.

I especially want to send a big thank you to the hundreds of people who helped me create and run all of my businesses. My former employees deserve most of the credit for the adventures that fill this book, but very few of their names are mentioned since this is a business how-to and not a memoir or bio.

Here are the names of some of these very special people: Charlie, Barb, Charlotte, Robin, Susan, Jim, Steve, Pam, Gwen, Carol, Sarah, Deb, Ann, Stef, Donmartin, Pam, Marge, Amy, Roger, Steve, Wendy, Shelley, Peter, Gabe. Mercy, Brie, Linda, Susan, Rod, Dave, Minda, Thor, Harry, Peter, Stas, Caleb, Kelly, Dave, Whitney, Sharon, Rosie, Robert, Pam, Janelle, Fernando, Dennis, Bev, Laura Guillermo, Ghislaine, Stuart, Al, Beth, Beth, Chris, Karyn, John, Leo, Suzie. Dan, Flora, Rob, Peter, Paul, Kim, Kim, Tom, Jackie, Zena, Abbey, Natalie, Kim, Anastasia, Sam, Liz, Ginger, Jen, Marie, Terry, Chris, Marjsa, Kate, Tina, Carrie, Beth, Trang, Dante, Melissa, Marcello, Erin, Kim, Gary, Robin, Christine, Jackie, Lars, Jose, Jim, Mara, Cindi, Kate, Carrie, John and Charles, Mim, and of course Sandy.

About the Authors

Stuart Skorman is the founder and former CEO of four innovative, trendsetting companies: Empire Video, Reel.com, Hungry-Minds.com, and Elephant Pharmacy. He is best known for pioneering new business models and marketing them to baby boomers. Before launching his career as a serial entrepreneur, Skorman was an executive at Bread & Circus, the Boston-based natural foods chain bought by Whole Foods in 1992.

Between working on revolutionary start-ups, Skorman mentors up-and-coming entrepreneurs and is writing his second book, *Stuart's MBA for Start-Ups Only*. Stuart lives in San Francisco with his wife, Diana, where he spends his spare time playing music, exploring nature, and studying ancient history.

Catherine Guthrie is an award-winning journalist whose work has appeared in dozens of national magazines. She is an active member of the American Society of Journalists and Authors and writes from her home in Bloomington, Indiana, where she lives with her partner, Mary, a professor at Indiana University.

Index

A

Accounting, 14–16

AD Hillyer Company, 49–50

Adrenaline addiction, 3–4, 40, 107, 109

Adventures: bicycle-tour, 63–70; high-stakes poker, 103–104; outdoor, 151–160

Aerosmith, 33

Aggressiveness, 114–115, 118, 119

Akron, Ohio: family business in, 11–15, 42–46; growing up in, 11–16, 106–107

Alaska, 66

Algebra, 14–16

Allen, H., 127

Allen, P., 126

Allman Brothers, 34

Almanacs, 59–60, 190

Alternative pharmacy, 162–181. *See also* Elephant Pharmacy

Amazon.com, 124, 134, 185, 186

"Anatomy of a Movie," 132–133

Anticorporate climates, 75, 76, 169

Apple, 129

Arrogance, 4, 113, 188

Attention, paying, 69

Authenticity: on Haight Street in 1967, 17–18; of James Montgomery, 28–29, 40

B

Baby boomers: career in marketing to, 166; hippie culture and, 3; holistic pharmacy concept and, 176; toy store concept and, 100

Backroom bribes, 14

Baez, J., 17, 19–20

Bankruptcy, of family business, 44–45, 48

Bay 101 casino, 107

Bay Area. *See* Berkeley; Marin County; San Francisco

Beatles, 95

Beck, J., 32–33

Beck, S., 98–99, 122, 123, 136, 137, 186, 191

Bellagio, 109

Berkeley, California: Elephant Pharmacy in, 163, 168–169, 172–174, 189; population characteristics of, 169; real estate in, 169, 179, 189; Reel.com store in, 124–125, 128, 135–136

Best Buy, 170–171

Bezos, J., 124, 132, 134, 185

Bicycle touring, 63–70

Bigalows Chemists, 171

Big-box store, 165–166, 177

Big-company mentality, 192

Birthday celebrations, 136–137

Blockbuster, 74–75, 78, 88, 123, 191; consultancy with, 98–99, 122; Empire Video negotiations with, 96–99, 102; Empire Video sale to, 102; Reel.com negotiation with, 136; seducing, 97–99

Bluffing, 110, 115–116

Bodine, C., 175–176

Books, at Elephant Pharmacy, 171–172

Bookstores, 84

Boston, Massachusetts: commercial real estate career in, 48–52; consulting in, 72; political campaign job in, 41–42; video store prospects in, *versus* Vermont, 74–75

Boston Chicken, 99

Boston Tea Party, 32–33

Boston University (BU): friends from, 19–21, 25; James Montgomery at, 24–25, 26–27; Skorman at, 18–21

Bottom line: need to focus on, 143–144, 184; second, for idealism, 149. *See also* Profitability

Brand and brand building: for Elephant Pharmacy, 172–174; for Hungry Minds.com, 147; individual *versus* coalition vision for, 90; for Miracle Mart, 11; for rock-and-roll band, 33–34. *See also* Image; Marketing; Public relations

Bread & Circus, 48, 50–61, 123, 179; background on, 50; lessons learned at, 53–57, 58–61; management of, 52–61, 166; Prospect Street location of, 51–52; real estate hunting for, 50–52; Whole Foods' purchase of, 50

British Columbia, 64, 157–158

Brown, J., 19–20

Buffalo Springfield, 174

Buffet, W., 112

Bullshit, 31–32

Burlington, Vermont, 81, 83–84

Burnout: preventing employee, 86; as rock-and-roll band manager, 36–37

Business: choosing a, 7, 73–74, 99–100, 138–139, 180–181, 187, 188; designing, 188–189; finance-ability of, 190. *See also* New business models; Start-ups

Business 101 paper, 18–19

Business 2.0, 129

Business models, new. *See* New business models

Business plan: budgeting for bad luck in, 111–112, 193; failure of

Hungry Minds.com and, 144–147; importance of profitability and, 143–144, 145–147, 184

Business school education, 62

Buzz, 129, 147

C

Caldwell-Winfield Blues Band, 24

California. *See* Berkeley; Marin County; San Francisco; Silicon Valley

Cambridge, Massachusetts: Bread & Circus in, 51–52; Harnett's Apothecary in, 164

Candor, 60–61

"Can't Buy Me Love," 95

Capitalism: college essay on, 19; gentle, 18

Capitalization: creativity and, 180; dot-com boom and, 134–135; of Elephant Pharmacy, 175–176; of Empire Video, 73, 78–79, 90–91; financial discipline and, 110; issues in, 190; of Reel.com, 123–127. *See also* Investors

Captain Bob, 158–160

Category killers, 165

Chain stores, national: Berkeley's antipathy toward, 169, 172–174; drugstore, 169, 172–174, 176–177, 178, 180; retail industry and, 42; Vermonters' antipathy toward, 75, 76; video, 74–75, 97, 102, 103

Charisma, of James Montgomery, 28–29

Cherry-picking, 80

Chess, 16–17

Chief Joseph Pass, Montana, 68–69

Children, video store experience for, 81–82

"Cinema U," 131
Cleanliness, 56–57
Clorox Company, 129
Clothing retailers, 52, 56
CMGI, 125–126
Coca-Cola, 11
Colorado: biking in, 69; Pharmaca in, 164, 165–166
Competition: attention from, 170–171; scaring the, 118; studying the, 115–116
Concept companies, 124
Confidence: building, on bicycle tour, 67, 70; losing, in poker, 110; luck *versus* talent and, 112–113; opportunism and, 114–115, 119; projecting, 26–28; self-awareness and, 113–114
Conservatism, 116–117, 118–119
Context, 108–109
Contradiction, embracing, 190–191
Corporate infrastructure, 178
Cosmetics, natural, 162, 174
Country-western music, 101
Creativity: compensating for lack of, 190–191; importance of execution *versus*, 59–60; in name selection, 89–90; new industries and, 74; for online video rental start-up, 123; reasons to avoid, 180–181; for video store start-up, 74, 89–90. *See also* New business models
Cross-country biking, 63–70
Culture fit: for health food stores, 54; for holistic pharmacy, 179
Customer education, at Elephant Pharmacy, 163, 165, 166–167, 171–172, 173, 177, 184. *See also* Educational businesses; Movie matchmaking

Customers: attracting and retaining, 77–78, 81–84, 87–88, 172–174; of Elephant Pharmacy, 165, 169, 171–174; of Empire Video, 77–78, 81–86, 87–88, 91–92; listening to, 31–33, 83, 91–92, 171–172; as potential employees, 55, 57
CVS Pharmacy, 175–176

D

Dawson City, 112
Deception, 117
Decision making: context in, 108–109; delegating, 104; emotion *versus* logic in, 138; opportunistic, 114–115, 119
Delegation, 104
Desperation, 6
Details, importance of image *versus*, 33–34
Dion, C., 159
Direction, loss of, 94–95
Discipline, 109–110, 185–186
Discount retail industry, 42. *See also* Miracle Mart
Display system, 167
Dolphins, 151–153, 156
Dot-com boom, 96, 112–113, 134–135, 136, 146, 190; implosion of, 144–145, 147–148
Dot-com businesses, 99, 113; concept companies and, 124; investors in, 123–127, 134–135; marketing of, 129–131; video rental, 122–139. *See also* Hungry Minds.com; Reel.com
Double bottom line, 149
Drawing power, 35–36
Drugstore businesses, 162–181; as Elephant Pharmacy investors,

175–176; interest of, in Elephant Pharmacy model, 170–171; store managers in, 165; traditional *versus* creative models of, 176–179, 180. *See also* Elephant Pharmacy

Dylan, B., 17, 174

E

Economies of scale, 178

Education director position, 179

Educational businesses, 166; content quality and, 146; of Hungry Minds.com, 142–149; as mission, 142–143; of Reel.com, 131; toy store idea for, 100, 187. *See also* Customer education; Hungry Minds.com; Movie matchmaking

Ego: entrepreneurial, 4, 5, 104; luck and, 112; overconfidence and, 113, 146; in poker, 113–114

Elephant Pharmacy, 161–181, 189; challenges of, 176–179; CEO hiring mistake at, 167–168, 185–186; classes at, 172, 173; customer education materials of, 166–167, 171–172, 173, 177, 184; customers of, 165, 169, 171–174; drugstore industry interest in, 170–171, 175–176; financial pressures of, 110, 171–172, 174–175, 179–180, 187; human resource challenges of, 178–179; imitations of, 170–171; investors in, 175–176; location of, 163, 167, 168–169, 179, 189; market research for, 116, 117, 164, 165–166; marketing of, 172–174, 178, 189; mistakes with, 167–170, 185; naming of, 38; offerings of, 171–172; opening

of, 2, 168, 169–170; post-opening changes at, 171–172; purchasing challenges of, 177; start-up team for, 166–167; store managers for, 55; technology at, 169–170, 178, 185; vision for, 162–163

Emotions: in decision making, 138; in entrepreneurship, 5–6, 138

Empire Video, 72–92, 166, 188, 189; Blockbuster negotiations with, 96–99; capitalization of, 73, 78–79, 90–91; concept of, 78; customer experience at, 81–86, 87; customer relationships at, 77–78, 86, 87–88, 91–92; employee attitude at, 31; employee roles at, 82–83; employee selection and training at, 86–87; expansion of, 78–81; lessons learned with, 88–91; letting go of, 96, 103; locations of, 74–76, 77, 79, 80–81, 109, 114–115; marketing of, 77–78, 80, 85–86; mistakes made at, 88–89, 101–102, 186; movie matchmaking at, 84–86, 87, 91–92, 99; naming of, 89–90; origins of, 72–76; request system of, 77; sale of, 91, 102

Employee selection and hiring: attitude and, 31, 54–55; at Bread & Circus, 53–57, 58–59; at Elephant Pharmacy, 167–168, 178–179, 185–186; at Empire Video, 86; lessons learned about, 54–57; of M.B.A.s, 62; skepticism in, 117, 185–186

Employee termination, 87, 149

Employee training, 86–87

Employees: of Empire Video, 82–83, 86–87; enthusiastic, 31, 54–55; of Hungry Minds.com, 148

Enthusiasm: employee, 31, 54–55; losing, 94

Entrepreneurs: business school education and, 62; contradictions of, 190–191; conversations with small-town, 65–66; "double bottom line" for, 149; emotions in, 5–6; lessons for, 4–7, 184–193; luck *versus* talent in, 112–113; qualities of, 4–7, 118–119; rules for winning as, 118–119; transition to being, 192–193. *See also* Serial entrepreneurship; Start-ups

Entry barriers, 73

Eq-life, 171

Eureka, Montana, 107–108

Evans Lake, British Columbia, 157–158

Execution, importance of, *versus* creativity, 59–60

Experience, prior. *See* Prior experience

F

Failure: fear of, 5; of Hungry Minds.com, 113, 144, 148–149, 184, 188. *See also* Mistakes

Fake towns, 66–67

Families, video store experience for, 81–82

Family business. *See* Miracle Mart

FBI, 98

Fear of failure, 5

Feedback, soliciting, 31–33

Financeability, 190

Financial backup, 193

Financial independence, 94, 136, 142

Flea markets, 43

Flexibility, 192

Flying blind, 187–188

Focus groups: for Elephant Pharmacy, 173; for rock-and-roll band, 32, 33

For Dummies books, 148

Foreign films, 83–84

Franklin, B., 144

Free phones, 82

"Free Vermont," 101

Freud, S., 95

Front-line experience: for getting to know customers, 91–92; in health food store, 53

Fun, 138

G

Gambling, 114. *See also* Poker, high-stakes

Game: knowing when to leave the, 110, 117–118, 186–187; picking one's, 107–109

Garron, B., 97–98, 102

Gates, B., 112

Gentle capitalism, 18

GeoCities, 125

Gestalt therapy, 95

Giving back, 142, 143, 144, 145, 149. *See also* Helping others

Glens Falls, New York, 81

Goals, short-term, 139

Goodyear Blimp, 129

Greed, 6

Greeting cards, 116, 172, 181

Grocery stores: components of quality, 36; conventional *versus* health-food, 50, 54, 57; real estate selection for, 50–52. *See also* Bread

& Circus; Health food stores;
Whole Foods Market
Guarantees, customer, 83

H
Haight Street, 3, 16–18, 122
Hard work, luck and, 112
Hardship, 7, 188–189
Harmonica playing, 24–25, 100–101
Harnett, A.: alternative pharmacy of,
164; battles with, 60–61, 72; initial
meetings with, 50–52; lessons
learned with, 57–61, 191; personality of, 57–58; as Reel.com
investor, 123
Harnett's Apothecary, 164
Health food, in Elephant Pharmacy,
172, 173–174
Health food stores: conventional
grocery stores *versus*, 50, 54, 57;
holistic pharmacy *versus*, 178;
human resources lessons for,
53–57, 58–59; lessons learned
with, 58–61; management of,
50–61; real estate for, 50–52. *See
also* Bread & Circus; Elephant
Pharmacy; Whole Foods Market
Health maintenance organizations
(HMOs), 176–177
Heart-and-soul business: poker
versus, 118; role models for, 29,
38, 50
Helping others: as business value, 13,
29, 142, 184; Hungry Minds.com
and, 142, 143, 144, 145; profit
focus and, 143–144, 149, 184;
second bottom line for, 149
Herbal pharmacy, 162–181. *See also*
Elephant Pharmacy

High-stakes poker. *See* Poker, high-
stakes
Highway patrolmen, Vermont, 103
Hills, biking on, 68–69
Hiring. *See* Employee selection and
hiring
Holiday shoppers, 170
Holistic pharmacy, 162–181. *See also*
Elephant Pharmacy
Hollywood Video, 125, 136
Honesty, importance of, 12–13, 60–61
Hoover, J. E., 98
Huizenga, W., 118
Human resources lessons, 53–57,
58–59, 178–179. *See also Employee*
headings
Humor, 12, 28
Hunger, 66–67
Hungry Minds.com, 141–149, 166;
business model of, 142–143, 147;
failure of, 113, 144, 148–149, 184,
186, 188; lack of business plan for,
144–145; media buzz for, 147;
office location of, 146; sale of, to
IDG Books, 148, 152

I
IBM, 99
Idaho, 66–67
Ideas. *See* Creativity; New business
models
IDG Books, 148
Image: business design for, 38; value
of, 27–28, 33–34. *See also* Brand
and brand building
IMDb (Internet Movie Database),
133–134, 185
Initial public offering (IPO), 135
Insanity, 4

Insurance, for Elephant Pharmacy, 177

Intel, 99

Internet: in early 1990s, 99; learning about, 122; in mid-1990s, 122. *See also* Dot-com boom; Dot-com businesses

Investors: attracting, 190; in dot-com era, 134–135; in Elephant Pharmacy, 175–176; in Empire Video, 89, 90–91; friends as, 90–91; in Reel.com, 123–127, 128. *See also* Capitalization

J

J. Geils Band, 20

Jamaica: fiftieth birthday celebration in, 137; music in, 100–101, 137

James Montgomery Band: concert success of, 33–36; management of, 25–38, 166, 188; recording failure of, 36–37; retirement from, 36–38, 40, 96

Jehovah's Witnesses, 157–158

J.J., 16–17, 191

Job descriptions: for Empire Video, 82–83; for health food stores, 54, 56–57

Job titles, juggling multiple, 52–53

Jobs, S., 112

Joy, 6

JP Morgan, 175

K

Keene, New Hampshire, 79, 80, 81, 88

Kerouac, J., 21

Kidney stones, 167, 168, 185

Kiosks, video, 99, 125, 128

Kmart, 42

L

Lagunitas, California, 40–41

Larson, S., 166

Las Vegas, 109

"Last Day Blues," 137

Late-fee collection system, 89, 186

Leadership: delegation and, 104; toughness in, 57–58, 61

Leap, being ready to, 114–115

Learning disability, 14

"Legend of Lionel Shapiro," 103

Lehto, M., 166

Leominster, Massachusetts, 81

Let's Make a Deal, 170

Letting go: of Empire Video, 96, 103; of mistakes, 7, 58–59; serial entrepreneurship and, 96

Life, 3, 16

Location: context and, 109; elements of, 75–76, 189; of Elephant Pharmacy, 163, 167, 168–169, 179, 189; of Empire Video stores, 74–76, 77, 79, 80–81, 109, 114–115; of Hungry Minds.com office, 146; importance of, 49, 74; of Reel.com office, 123, 124; of Reel.com store, 124–125

Loneliness, 95

Longs, 171

Love life, 95

Luck: gambling and, 114; planning for bad, 111–112, 193; talent *versus,* 112–113

Lycos, 125

Lyme disease, 159–160

M

Macrobiotic diet, 58

Maltin, L., 85

Manchester Center, Vermont, 75–76, 77, 79, 85, 114–115

Map publishers, 66–67

Marin County, California, 40–41

Market research: for holistic pharmacy, 164, 165–166; for online learning, 145; for rock-and-roll band management, 32–33; for start-ups, 116–117, 138, 188

Marketing: of Elephant Pharmacy, 172–174, 178, 189; of Empire Video, 77–78, 80, 85–86; of Hungry Minds.com, 147; of Miracle Mart, 11; of Reel.com, 126, 129–131; in rock-and-roll business, 33–36. See also Brand; Press; Public relations

Massachusetts. See Boston, Massachusetts; Cambridge, Massachusetts

Mathematics: business, 14–16; of supply and demand, 34–36

M.B.A.s, 62

McDonald's, 76, 114

Media businesses, new versus old releases in, 85

Melon-headed whales, 153–154

Mentor(s), 191; Anthony Harnett as, 57–61; importance of, 21; James Montgomery as, 24–25, 28–29, 38; Scott Beck as, 99; selecting and relating with, 21–22

Mentoring others, 22

Microsoft, 126

Miller, S., 34

Millionaire, being a, 94

Mills, P., 125

Miracle Mart, 2, 82; demise of, 42–46, 48; management of, 42–46; in Skorman's childhood, 11–15

Mistakes: with Elephant Pharmacy, 167–170, 185–186; with Empire Video, 88–89, 101–102, 186; learning from, 7, 59, 184; lessons learned from, 184–193; letting go of, 7, 58–59; with Reel.com, 131–134; in technology management, 88–89, 131–133, 169–170, 185, 186. See also Failure

Money, 143

Money management, 109–110, 147–148

Montana, 68–69

Montgomery, J.: authenticity of, 28–30, 40; harmonica lessons with, 24–25; later meeting with, 37–38; lessons learned from, 27, 28–30, 35, 191

Motivation, for becoming an entrepreneur, 192

Motorcycle gang, 68–69

Mountains: biking in, 68–69; in British Columbia, 157–158

"Movie expert" job, 82–83

Movie matchmaking: at Empire Video, 84–86, 87, 91–92; health information and, 167; at Reel.com, 122, 128, 132–133; with technology, 99, 122, 132–133

Movie recommendation systems, 82–83, 84–86. See also Movie matchmaking

Movie reviews, online, 128, 130–131, 132–133

Murphy's law, 111

Musician(s): business savvy in, 29; drawing power of, 35–36; recording and, 36–37; Skorman as, 24–25, 100–101; supply and demand for, 34–35

N

Name selection: aspects of, 38; for Elephant Pharmacy, 38; for Empire Video, 89–90

National chains. *See* Chain stores, national

National-scale business, aspirations for, 95, 96

Natural foods. *See* Health food; Health food stores

Negotiation, 115–116

Neihaus Ryan Wong, 129

Netflix, 133

Nevis, S., 95–97, 103, 191

New business models: caution with, 116–117, 138, 145–146, 165, 176, 180–181, 187–188; creativity and, 74, 180–181; holistic pharmacy as, 162–163, 165–166, 170–171, 176–179, 180–181; online education portal as, 142–143, 147; online video rental as, 123; risk level of, 138–139. *See also* Creativity

New Hampshire, 79, 80, 81, 88

New *versus* older releases, 85–86, 87

New York City: Garment District, 11, 13–14; trading in, 72

New York State, Empire Video in, 80–81, 89

New York Times, 60, 72

Nike, 167

Noodle Kadoodle, 100

O

Ogilvy, D., 181

Ohio. *See* Akron, Ohio

Online businesses. *See* Dot-com businesses; Hungry Minds.com; Reel.com

Online learning portal, 141–149. *See also* Hungry Minds.com

Operations expertise, 43–44, 53, 128–129

Opponents, understanding, 115–117. *See also* Competition

Opportunism, 114–115, 119

Ordering system, online, 133

Outdoor travel adventures, 151–160

Out-of-the-box thinking, 180–181. *See also* Creativity; New business models

Overconfidence, 113–114, 146

P

Parking considerations, 75

Passion: being blinded by, 163, 164–166; of entrepreneurs, 6, 138

People, reading, 115–117

People's Almanac, The, 60, 190

Perdue, F., 58

Perks: customer, 82; employee, 86

Perseverance, 67–69

Persistence, 67–69

Personality: business choice and, 138; tough, 57–58, 61; for video retailing, 74

Pharmaca, 164, 165–166, 171

Pharmacy business. *See* Drugstore businesses; Elephant Pharmacy

Plattsburgh, New York, 81

Players, playing the, 115–117

Poetry, 18, 21

Poker, high-stakes, 4, 103–104; as business training ground, 106; career in, 106–119; flying blind in, 187–188; gambling *versus,* 114;

learning, 106–107; lessons learned with, 107–119; picking one's game in, 107–109; rules to winning in, 118–119

Policies, 192

Political campaign job, 41–42

Popcorn, 82

Portal, online learning, 141–149

Poughkeepsie, New York, 81

Prescription-driven business model, 177, 178, 180

Press: business design for, 38; for Hungry Minds.com, 147; importance of good, 34; for Reel.com, 129, 131. *See also* Marketing; Public relations

Pricing system, 169–170

Prior experience: in hiring, 55; importance of, for new business venture, 100, 188; for video store business, 73

Professional organizations, 22

Profitability: doing good and, 143–144, 149, 184; importance of business planning for, 143–144, 145–147; of Reel.com, 125, 134–135; of video store business, 73, 85, 87–88

Promotions: at Elephant Pharmacy, 173; at Empire Video, 85–86; of Reel.com, 130

Psychotherapy, 95–97, 103, 191

Public relations: business design and, 38; for Empire Video, 78; for Hungry Minds.com, 147; for Reel.com, 126, 129–131; small towns and, 78. *See also* Brand; Marketing; Press

Pullout display system, 167

Purchasing, at Elephant Pharmacy, 177

R

Raising Arizona, 92

Raitt, B., 34

Rasher, D., 133

Reagan, R., 54–55

Real estate: career in, 48–52, 190; obtaining, 80, 166; in San Francisco Bay Area, 169, 179, 189; for start-ups, 179. *See also* Location

Real estate brokers, 49–50, 80

Recording business, 36–37

Reel.com, 99, 113, 122–139, 166; business model of, 123, 124–125, 127–128; CEO of, 128–129; Hollywood Video buyout of, 125, 136; IMDb and, 133–134, 185; investors in, 123–127, 128; mail-order business of, 127–128, 133; marketing of, 126, 129–131; movie information business of, 128, 130–131, 132–134; office location of, 123, 124; physical store of, 124–125, 128, 135–136; profitability of, 125, 134–135; technology management of, 126, 131–133, 186

Reggae, 101

Religious fanatics, 157–158

Request system, video, 77

Résumé, delegating to the person with the best, 104

Retail business: location and, 49, 74–75; national chains and, 42; real estate and, 48–52; store managers and, 55. *See also* Drugstore businesses; Elephant Pharmacy;

Grocery stores; Health food stores; Miracle Mart; Video store business
Retirement risk, 162, 175, 179, 187
Richert, K., 187–188
Risk taking: on bicycle tour, 69, 70; in investment, 110, 162, 175; in poker, 109–110; in serial entrepreneurship, 70, 184
Risk tolerance, 138–139
Rite Aid, 171
Roadies, 31
Rock-and-roll band management, 25–38. See also James Montgomery Band
Rumination, 123
Russo, A., 20

S
Safety issues, 56–57
San Francisco: Elephant Pharmacy office in, 166; Hungry Minds.com office in, 146; move to, 122; poker in, 107; Reel.com office in, 123, 124; South Park, 124; Summer of Love (1967) in, 3, 16–18, 122
San Rafael, Elephant Pharmacy in, 163
Santa Fe, New Mexico, 171, 189
SAT scores, 18
Sea snakes, 155–156
Second bottom line, 149
Security access, concert, 26–27
Selection. See Employee selection and hiring
Self-assurance, projecting, 27–28. See also Confidence
Self-awareness, 113–114, 190–191
Self-employment, 192
Self-exploration, 94–97, 99–100, 103, 191

Serial entrepreneurship: hardships of, 7, 188–189; letting go and, 96; risk taking and, 70, 184
Severance pay, 149
Shapiro, L., 103
Sharks, 156
Shelving systems, 81, 171–172
Short-term goals, 139
Sickley, S., 142, 143, 166, 185–186
Silicon Valley, 122, 132, 134
Skagway, Alaska, 66
Skepticism, 79, 117
Skorman, M., 95
Skorman, S. (Simon), 10–11, 106–107
Skorman, S. (Stuart): bicycle-touring adventures of, 63–70; Blockbuster consultancy of, 98–99; at Bread & Circus, 50–61; brother of, 95, 123; childhood of, 3, 10–16, 106–107; in college, 18–21; early education of, 3, 14–16; in family business, 2–3, 10–16, 42–46, 48; father of, 11–15, 42, 45, 46, 48, 137; fiftieth birthday party of, 136–137; grandfather of, 10–11, 106–107; as grown-up, 45–46; in high-stakes poker, 103–104, 106–119; holistic pharmacy start-up of, 161–181; in Jamaica, 100–101; as millionaire, 93; mother of, 15–16, 42, 129–130; as musician, 19–20, 24–25; online education portal start-up of, 141–149; online video start-up of, 121–139; outdoor adventures of, 151–160; political campaign job of, 41–42; in real estate business, 48–52; as rock-and-roll band manager, 25–38; in San Francisco, 3, 16–18, 122; self-exploration of, 94–97, 99–100, 103, 191; in

Vermont, 20–21, 72, 74–76, 100, 102–103; video store start-up of, 72–92; Wall Street trading of, 72; wife (Diana) of, 96, 137, 159–160

Slogans, 66

Slowing down: costs of not, 133–134, 144–145; methods of, 185–186; value of, 65–66, 185–186

Small, starting, 138

Snorkeling, 155–156, 159

Snyder, J., 127

Social responsibility, 149. *See also* Helping others

Solon, M., 100–101

Sourcing, for Elephant Pharmacy, 177

South Pacific adventures, 4, 152–156

Sprinter, 37

Stalin, J., 19

Star Wars, 89–90

Start-ups: business school education and, 62; choosing a business for, 7, 73–74, 99–100, 138–139; emotional aspects of, 5–6; holistic pharmacy, 162–181; lessons for entrepreneurs and, 4–7, 184–193; making the transition to, 192–193; market research for, 116–117; online education portal, 142–149; online video rental, 121–139; overview of Skorman's, 3; poker lessons applied to, 107–119; relevant experience prerequisite for, 100; team building for, 166–167; video store, 71–92; winning strategies for, 118–119. *See also* Entrepreneurs

Status quo, questioning the, 18–19

Stewart, R., 32–33

Stock market, 72, 135

Store managers: for Bread & Circus, 54, 58–59; for Elephant Pharmacy, 165; hiring, 55–56, 58–59; importance of, 55

Strengths, understanding one's, 113–114, 190–191

Summer of Love, 3, 16–18, 122

Super Bowl commercials, 129

Supply and demand, in music business, 34–36

Support, importance of, 6

Surprise gifts, for customers, 82

T

Tagline, 38

Talent *versus* luck, 112–113

Tarantino, Q., 92

Taxi driver job, 25, 26

Teachers, free video rentals for, 78

Techies, 88, 132, 146, 169, 186

Technology: at Blockbuster, 99; at Elephant Pharmacy, 169–170, 178; at Empire Video, 88–89; learning about, 99; mistakes in managing, 88–89, 131–133, 169–170, 185, 186; for movie matchmaking, 99, 122, 132–133; at Reel.com, 126, 131–133, 186; revolution in, 99

Terror, 5

The Limited, 171

Tiger sharks, 156

Tight, playing, 118–119

Time requirements: of entrepreneurship, 6–7, 30, 103, 188–189; of rock-band management, 30

Titanic promotion, 130

Toughness, 57–58, 61

Town Taxi, 25

Toy store idea, 100, 187

Trading, 72

Turtles, 155

U

Udall, M., 41–42
Uncle Lou, 20, 25–26, 27
Underachiever, in school, 14, 18
University of California at Berkeley extension, 143
University of Phoenix, 145

V

Venture capitalists, 125–126. *See also* Capitalization; Investors
Vermont: Act 250 of, 76; Empire Video start-up in, 72–92; people and culture of, 102–103; Skorman in, 20–21, 72, 74–76, 100, 102–103; small-business climate in, 75, 76, 78
Vermont Secessionist Blues Band, 101
Viacom, 102
Video categories, 81
Video Store, 81, 97
Video store business: chain, 74–75; Empire, 71–92; lessons learned with, 88–91; location selection for, 74–76, 77, 79, 80–81, 109, 114–115; online, 121–139; profitability of, 73, 85, 87–88; reasons for choosing, 73–74, 111, 188; Reel.com, 121–139; technology in, 88–89. *See also* Blockbuster; Empire Video; Reel.com
Vonnegut, K., 21

W

Wainwright, J., 128–129, 130, 134, 136
Walgreens, 116, 170, 173, 178, 180, 181

Wall Street trading, 72
Wal-Mart, 42, 75
Warren Indoor Flea Market, 43
Waste Management, 118
Weaknesses, understanding one's, 113–114, 190–191
Weather, video rentals and, 78, 79
Web site: crashes, 131–133; of Hungry Minds.com, 146; of Reel.com, 131–133. *See also* Dot-com businesses; Hungry Minds.com; Internet; Reel.com
Wellness information and classes, 163, 165, 166–167, 171–172, 173, 177
Wetherall, D., 125
Whales, 153–154
Whole Foods Market, 164, 176, 178; Bread & Circus purchase by, 50; quality components of, 36; store managers of, 55
Wild Oats, 171
Wind, changeability of, 67–69
Winning strategies, 118–119
Winter, E., 34
Wired, 122, 129, 132
Wizard of Oz, 124
Writer, Skorman as, 40–41, 45, 128
Writing, for Reel.com, 128, 130–131

Y

Yacht trip, 158–159
Yahoo!, 129
Yes people, 33

Z

Zen Judaism, 174